Godly Rule

POLITICS AND RELIGION, 1603–1660

Godly Rule

POLITICS AND RELIGION, 1603-60

William M. Lamont

MACMILLAN
ST MARTIN'S PRESS

© William M. Lamont 1969

First published 1969 by
MACMILLAN AND CO LTD
Little Essex Street London WC2
and also at Bombay Calcutta and Madras
Macmillan South Africa (Publishers) Pty Ltd
Johannesburg
The Macmillan Company of Australia Pty Ltd
Melbourne
The Macmillan Company of Canada Ltd Toronto
St Martin's Press Inc New York
Gill and Macmillian Ltd Dublin

Library of Congress catalog card no. 69–20439

Printed in Great Britain by
RICHARD CLAY (THE CHAUCER PRESS) LTD
Bungay, Suffolk

To my Father and Mother

Contents

Acknowledgements

When one reads examination scripts of candidates specialising in English history of the seventeenth century, whether they are sixth-formers, College of Education students, or University students, one swiftly enters a twilight world where King James I is for ever haranguing his rebellious subjects about royal absolutism, where Archbishop Laud is for ever prostrating himself before the throne, where Erastianism is cynicism and millenarianism is fanaticism. Mr Philip Whitting first encouraged me to believe that there was a place for a modest little essay on the political and religious controversies of the time which threw into question some of these bland assumptions. *Godly Rule* is the result; although he cannot be held responsible for any failure to achieve these aims. I wish to acknowledge help from the following libraries: Doctor Williams's Library; the British Museum; the Public Record Office; the House of Lords Record Office. The Editors of *History Today* have an enviable reputation for encouraging young writers, and some of the points made in my third and fourth chapters were first developed in that journal (volumes 14 and 16 respectively). My sister heroically wrestled with my handwriting and typed the entire draft.

University of Sussex   W.M.L.
September 1968

A Note on Terminology

The *Apocalypse* is the revelation of the future which was granted to St John in the Isle of Patmos. *Millenarianism* (often used interchangeably with *chiliasm*) is the term used to describe the belief in the imminence of that period of a thousand years, described in the twentieth chapter of the Book of Revelation, when a messianic kingdom is established on earth.

One valuable insight which we have gained from recent research into seventeenth-century thought has been the recognition that the term 'millenarianism' has been given too limited an interpretation. It has been too often in the past used exclusively of those activists who themselves set out to establish that messianic kingdom. Among millenarians they were certainly a minority. Strictly speaking, there could be two developments of millenarianism: *pre-millennial* and *post-millennial* belief. The first assumed that the Second Coming of Christ would precede the millennium; the second, that the millennium would come first and that the Second Coming would occur at the *end* of this process. Most of the English writers of the seventeenth century that are described in this book are pre-millennial. But within the ranks of those holding pre-millennial beliefs further divisions are possible: between those who emphasise the *spiritual* nature of the Resurrection, those who emphasise the *literal* nature of the Resurrection but are hazy about details of the future kingdom, and those who emphasise the *literal* nature of the Resurrection and are precise about the characteristics of the future kingdom. The political activists were to be found in the third category, but do not even there represent a majority view. L. F. Solt has shown ('The Fifth Monarchy Men: Politics and the Millennium', *Church*

History, 30, 1961) that only a minority of Fifth Monarchy Men followed Venner in feeling an obligation to translate their vision of the future into concrete revolutionary activity *now*.

Winstanley, Milton and Hobbes are three writers who can be looked at afresh in the light of this insight. Winthrop Hudson ('Economic and Social Thought of Gerrard Winstanley', *Journal of Modern History*, 18, 1946) has argued persuasively the view that Winstanley's Digger programme owed more to the Book of Revelation than to Karl Marx. Michael Fixler – in a book which was consulted too late for use in this study, *Milton and the Kingdom of God* (London, 1964) – has argued that Milton's millenarianism survived even his distaste for Fifth Monarchy political activity, and that *Paradise Regained* is his rebuke to the Saints – unlike Job – who would not wait for the Kingdom of Christ to come. Hobbes – with his hearty contempt for allegorical readings of the Book of Revelation – seems a paradoxical figure to be included here but John Pocock (who has allowed me to see the typescript of an essay on Hobbes which is about to be published) has argued brilliantly for the view that Books III and IV of *Leviathan* are prophetic books within the mainstream of post-millennial belief.

These are revisions that have been made possible by a much more generous reading of the term 'millenarianism' than was common in the past. This study borrows that insight to offer a reinterpretation of political and religious controversies in the first half of the seventeenth century. But – compared to these revisions – its aims are much lower. It does not pretend to be a systematic analysis of millenarian thought in the seventeenth century. There may well be a place for such a study and, if it does come to be written, it will need to bring a comparable rigour and detail to that which has been applied to Winstanley, Milton and Hobbes.

Now that we are coming to realise how widely eschatological preconceptions pervaded English intellectual life in the seventeenth century, there is need to reappraise the traditional controversies of the period before and after the Civil War. This is what I have attempted to do in this study and I have used terms such as *Apocalypse, millenarianism* and *chiliasm* in a non-purist sense; in the sense in which, in fact, Sylvia Thrupp used them in her introduction to a comparative study on millenarian movements (*Millennial Dreams in Action,* The Hague, 1962) as applying 'figuratively to any conception of a perfect age to come, or of a perfect land to be made accessible'.

That is why – both in the title and throughout the text – I have used such a deliberately vague term as 'Godly Rule' to describe that vision of the future society. If older historians applied the term 'millenarianism' to too narrow a grouping, I may well be accused of erring in the opposite direction: of interpreting it too widely. This risk I have taken in the belief that the time has come for at least an interim judgement on the way that our traditional version of political and religious controversies may come to be modified by the recognition of the grip that eschatology had on the minds of Englishmen in the early seventeenth century.

5 March 1969   W.M.L.

The Protagonists

For a 'Godly Rule'

WILLIAM PRYNNE (1600–69): Puritan pamphleteer; barrister, Lincoln's Inn; ears mutilated twice (1634 and 1637) for his attacks on Laudian bishops; Keeper of the Records in the Tower of London and M.P. for Bath after the Restoration.

For a 'Godly Prince'

JOHN FOXE (1516–87): Marian exile; author of *Acts and Monuments*, popularly known as *The Book of Martyrs*.

JOHN JEWEL (1522–71): Marian exile; bishop of Salisbury; author of *Defence of the Apology*.

JOHN REYNOLDS (1549–1607): leading Puritan at the Hampton Court Conference; president of Corpus Christi College, Oxford.

JOHN WILLIAMS (1582–1650): bishop of Lincoln and archbishop of York; Laud's greatest enemy *within* the ranks of the Church of England.

JAMES USHER (1581–1656): archbishop of Armagh; drafted a scheme of modified episcopacy in 1641 which was acceptable to some Puritans.

For a 'Godly Bishop'

RICHARD BANCROFT (1544–1610): archbishop of Canterbury and author of the first plea for episcopacy by divine right.

THOMAS BILSON (1547–1616): bishop of Winchester; popular with Parliamentary apologists in the English Civil War.

GEORGE CARLETON (1559–1628): bishop of Chichester; represented the Church of England (on the Calvinist side) at the Synod of Dort, 1618–19.

GEORGE DOWNAME (d. 1634): bishop of Derry; anti-Arminian.

WILLIAM BARLOW (d. 1613): bishop of Lincoln; drew up the report of the Hampton Court Conference.

WILLIAM LAUD (1573–1645): archbishop of Canterbury; beheaded for treason by the Long Parliament.

PETER HEYLYN (1600–62): Laud's first biographer; *Cyprianus Anglicus* was his attempt at rehabilitating his master's reputation.

JOSEPH HALL (1574–1656): bishop of Exeter and Norwich; once identified with Calvinist opponents of Laud but made handsome redress with his defence of episcopacy by divine right in 1640.

RICHARD MOUNTAGUE (1577–1641): bishop of Chichester; the leading Arminian apologist on doctrinal matters.

JOHN COSIN (1594–1672): bishop of Durham; friend of Laud and Mountague.

For a 'Godly People'

THOMAS BRIGHTMAN (1562–1607): Bedfordshire rector; most influential millenarian writer.

JOHN BASTWICK (1593–1654): physician and fellow-victim with Prynne in 1637; a committed Presbyterian.

HENRY BURTON (1578–1648): minister and fellow-victim with Prynne in 1637; a committed Independent.

STEPHEN MARSHALL (1594–1655): the most powerful of the London 'root and branch' ministers; co-author of the pamphlets against Joseph Hall under the title of Smectymnuus (Stephen Marshall, Edmund Calamy, Thomas Young, Matthew Newcomen, William Spurstowe).

THOMAS CASE (1598–1682): another influential London 'root and branch' minister; chaplain to Charles II at his Restoration but subsequently ejected from his living under the Clarendon Code.

CORNELIUS BURGES (1589–1665): a 'root and branch' minister who opposed the imposition of the Covenant in 1643.

RICHARD BAXTER (1615–91): Puritan chaplain in Roundhead Army; attempted reconciliation between Anglicans and Puritans in the Interregnum and immediately after the Restoration; victimised in the reigns of Charles II and James II.

EDWARD DERING (1598–1644): M.P. for Kent in the Long Parliament; moved the first reading of the Root and Branch Bill but made a spectacular recantation a month later.

MATTHEW HOPKINS (d. 1647): the notorious witch-finder; made journeys for discovery of witches in eastern counties and Huntingdonshire, 1644–7; hanged as a sorcerer.

For a 'Godly Parliament'

THOMAS COLEMAN (1598–1647): Lincolnshire rector and member of the Westminster Assembly; the leading Erastian pamphleteer.

For a 'Godless Rule'

ROGER WILLIAMS (1604–83): New England divine and pioneer of religious freedom.

GEORGE FOX (1624–91): founder of the Quakers and author of *Journal*.

JOHN SELDEN (1584–1654): jurist and antiquarian; an uncomfortable member of the Assembly of Divines; notorious for his anti-clericalism.

GILBERT SHELDON (1598–1677): archbishop of Canterbury; not an intimate friend of Laud but a key member of the 'Laudian' group who captured the ecclesiastical government after the Restoration.

JOHN TILLOTSON (1630–94): archbishop of Canterbury and apologist for the Latitudinarian case that prevailed near the end of the seventeenth century in England.

Introduction

Millenarianism has been too often dismissed as a creed for cranks. When Sylvia Thrupp brought together an important collection of comparative studies on this theme in 1962, *Millennial Dreams in Action,* she noted the traditional heavy bias in the literature of the subject towards 'the more dramatic types of movement, those that alarm civil and religious authorities or openly clash with them'. But she was impressed, on the contrary, by the *normalcy* of millennial movements; that, for instance, the recent history of Brazil demonstrated that 'a belief that the end of the world is imminent may cause excitement and call for certain decisive actions, without any spirit of anxiety'.

Because we assume that millenarianism is abnormal we *expect* to find a spirit of anxiety among millenarians. We may interpret this in different ways. We may see it as the failure of the individual to adjust to society. We may see it as the failure of a society at a given time to respond to intolerable pressures on it. In other words, we may psychoanalyse John of Leyden, or we may explain the exceptional social and political factors that made a John of Leyden possible. But what if our original premise is wrong? What if millenarianism meant not alienation from the spirit of the age but a total involvement with it?

This is the question that I want to ask of England in the first half of the seventeenth century. This can be the only justification for another survey of English political and religious history from the accession of James I to the restoration of Charles II. The need to look at those years afresh is suggested by Professor Hugh Trevor-Roper's essay, 'The European Witch-Craze', which has recently been published in his *Religion, The Reformation and*

Social Change (Macmillan, 1967). Professor Trevor-Roper recognises that 'the mind of one age is not necessarily subject to the same rules as the mind of another'. We may understand the appeal of the witch-craze to the knave and to the fool, but to Bodin – 'the Aristotle, the Montesquieu of the sixteenth century'? We may understand the appeal of the witch-craze to a society disordered by the Black Death and the Hundred Years War, but why is it at its peak in 'two centuries not of misery but of European recovery and expansion'? Professor Trevor-Roper believes that the resilience of the witch-craze is due to the fact that it *complemented*, not *challenged*, the mind of the age. Thus, even when men 'revolted against the cruelty of torture, against the implausibility of confessions, against the identification of witches', they 'did not revolt against the central doctrine of the kingdom of Satan and its war on humanity by means of demons and witches'. He believes then that the witch-craze is inextricably linked with the revival of millenary ideas: 'all through the sixteenth and seventeenth centuries it had been an axiom of faith that the Church was engaged in a life-and-death struggle with Satan'. And it is notable that he calls this concept 'a *central* doctrine'. Acute social and political tensions may explain why in 1645 more witches were executed in England than in any year before or since, but no theory of *maladjustment* (personal or social) will explain away the fact that witch-hunting finds its champions in England among such non-peripheral figures as Bishop Jewel (informing Queen Elizabeth that witches and sorcerers 'within these last few years are marvellously increased within this your Grace's realm'), William Perkins and King James I himself.

Only a theory of *adjustment* will resolve the paradox: that burning of witches came easily to men who already believed that they were locked in a struggle with Antichrist. That is why Professor Trevor-Roper is right to see Bishop Jewel's counsel to Elizabeth as a Protestant declaration of war upon 'the Catholic England of Mary Tudor'. The conviction that the end of the world was imminent and that the Roman Church was Antichrist: this was held by both Bishop Jewel and by James I. It could lead, as Sylvia Thrupp saw, to excitement and to decisive actions (the burning of witches?), but it need not lead to anxiety. Indeed, there was a very good reason why it should not lead to anxiety: the Book of Revelation had foretold the destruction of Antichrist. How far such confidence was widespread among English Protestants in the first half of the seventeenth century; how important were the effects of such a belief on their actions; when and why this confidence was eroded: these are the questions that this book will attempt to answer.

1 Godly Rule

> The last glimpse of the Godlike vanishing from this England; conviction and veracity giving place to hollow cant and formalism antique 'Reign of God,' which all true men in their several dialects and modes have always strived for, giving place to modern Reign of the no-God; who men name Devil: this, in its multitudinous meanings and results, is a sight to create reflections in the earnest man! One wishes there were a History of English Puritanism, the last of all our Heroisms; but sees small prospect of such a thing at present.[1]

Thomas Carlyle saw Oliver Cromwell as the 'last glimpse of the Godlike vanishing from this England'. He believed that his fellow-Victorians could not share Cromwell's intimations because too many of them now worshipped 'the no-God'. The Victorians were not pure enough to understand the puritans of the seventeenth century. We would see it differently: that it was the Victorians' puritanism, not their impurity, that blocked an understanding of their ancestors. For what is striking in Carlyle's passage is the implicit assumption that the antique 'Reign of God' which Cromwell was striving for was the same 'Reign of God' which the true men *of his own time* were striving for. Since the time of Carlyle we have never been able to slay this assumption. We talk about 'the Puritan Revolution' and think about Victorian nonconformity. As Christopher Hill says, 'they differ as much as vinegar does from wine'.[2] Mr Gladstone can share with Cromwell trouble with the Crown, the Irish and his syntax, but remains crucially different. If we turn from Carlyle and Gladstone to one of their near-contemporaries, this difference may become clearer.

Edmund Gosse has hauntingly described his Victorian child-hood: of the comfort which he and his devout father derived from turning to the Book of Revelation and chasing 'the phantom of Popery through its ... fuliginous pages'. The Apocalypse bound together father and son:

> Hand in hand we investigated the number of the Beast, which number is six hundred three score and six. Hand in hand we inspected the nations, to see whether they had the mark of Babylon in their foreheads. Hand in hand we watched the spirits of devils gathering the kings of the earth into the place which is called in the Hebrew tongue Armageddon.

Gosse felt that this gave a cutting edge to his hatred of Popery. The anti-Catholic bigots of his day lacked the oceanic dread which the Papacy inspired in a man who could decipher the Apocalypse:

> I regarded it with a vague terror as a wild beast, the only good point about it being that it was very old and was soon to die.

When would it die? Gosse described his father's ordeal:

> He awaited, with anxious hope, 'the coming of the Lord', an event which he still frequently believed to be imminent. He would calculate, by reference to prophecies in the Old and New Testament, the exact date of this event: the date would pass, without the expected Advent, and he would be more than disappointed – he would be incensed. Then he would under-stand that he must have made some slight error in calcula-tion, and the pleasures of anticipation would recommence.[3]

Uncannily Gosse has captured the experience of seventeenth-century English Protestantism: his father is an authentic Jaco-bean figure. His father is not an authentic Victorian figure: far from belonging to the mainstream of religious orthodoxy, he was a member of the Plymouth Brethren. By his time millenarian-ism belonged to the cranks. This was not true of the seventeenth century. What one misses in Victorian nonconformity is pre-cisely the sense of chiliastic chill: it is the difference between vinegar and wine.

Perhaps this difference is being overdrawn. It is true that
millenarianism is a powerful influence in the thought of the
seventeenth century, but did it ever extend much further than
Gosse's beliefs did in his own time? The Victorians had their
Plymouth Brethren; the seventeenth century had its Ranters and
Fifth Monarchy Men. But there is one towering difference: the
philosophical assumptions (though not the political conclusions
drawn from them) of the Fifth Monarchy Men were acceptable
to the orthodox mainstream of the religious thought of the time,
in a way that those of the Plymouth Brethren were not for *their*
time. The political conclusions of minority groups such as the
Ranters, Muggletonians and Fifth Monarchy Men were so spec-
tacularly divergent from the orthodox mainstream that their
philosophical *convergence* with orthodoxy has tended to be
obscured. We have a rich store of information about the millenarian radical groups: men who were convinced from their reading of the Book of Revelation that the end of the world was
imminent, Antichrist was about to be overthrown, the reign of
King Jesus was about to start. Such men naturally produced
propaganda for their beliefs: New Jerusalems abound. But our
concern in this study is with a quieter sort of men; men who
were no less millenarian but who did not see why the forthcoming end of the world should mean the forthcoming end of traditional political allegiances. Their millenarian faith was implicit;
there was no reason why it should be made explicit. For that
reason, it is extraordinarily difficult to track down. This study
is an attempt to hunt for this subtler form of millenarianism, but
the quarry is elusive. When a weirdie like Hannah Trapnel in
1654 proclaimed in verse her expectations of the Fifth Monarchy,
and pronounced that Cromwell was the Little Horn, there is no
danger of overrating the importance to her of millenarianism.[4]
When one is dealing with the tacit millenarians of this study there
is, however, a great danger of ascribing too much to the isolated
phrase torn out of context. But the alternative seems no less dangerous: of playing down the importance of this implicit millenarianism in the thinking of English Protestants in the first half
of the seventeenth century. The first half, not the second half:

for the second main argument of this study is that this implicit millenarianism ceases to be a formative influence on English Protestantism by the time of the Protectorate. In other words, this study accepts Carlyle's belief that Cromwell's rule was indeed a watershed, though not for the reasons that Carlyle gives. Nor for the reasons that Hannah Trapnel gave either: one can believe that by the end of Cromwell's rule the majority of English Protestants had abandoned the search for the 'Reign of God' without believing that Cromwell, therefore, *was* the Little Horn.

Was there a decisive change after Cromwell? James II had an exalted concept of kingship. So had James I. Archbishop Sheldon had an exalted concept of the Church of England. So had Archbishop Whitgift, and they both persecuted Puritans to prove it. The difference lies not in their *actions* but in their *aspirations*. James II did not base his claims for monarchy upon the Book of Revelation; James I did. Sheldon was, according to the Oxford historian Wood, 'the first who publicly denied the pope to be antichrist' in Oxford. He dared to affirm this when he was being examined for his thesis and shocked his examiner, Dr Prideaux.[5] Contrast this with Whitgift, whose doctoral dissertation was on the thesis that the Pope *was* Antichrist. But in 1589 the fourth examination of the Puritan, Henry Barrow, revealed one man who had not been swayed by Whitgift's thesis. When the Lord Chancellor pointed to Whitgift and asked Barrow who he was, Barrow replied:

> The Lord gave me the spirit of boldness, so that I answered: He is a monster, a miserable compound, I know not what to make [call] him: he is neither ecclesiastical nor civil, even that second beast spoken of in the Revelation.[6]

Poor Whitgift! Not often does one have one's doctoral dissertation so rudely inverted. Yet it is Whitgift's thesis, not Barrow's rudeness, that causes us surprise. We have grown accustomed to the link between radical sectarians like Barrow and millenarian views; but it is something of the nature of a paradox to find – in the age before Cromwell at least – kings and archbishops deriving spiritual (and political) comfort from the Apocalypse.

This should cause us less surprise than it does: we underrate the extraordinary mental agility of English Protestants in the reign of Elizabeth and the early Stuarts. They could tease out of the Book of Revelation the meanings that they wanted to tease out. One pamphleteer in 1676 shrewdly realised as much: Hayter's own contribution to apocalyptic learning, *A Meaning to the Revelation*, was in other respects unremarkable, but his preface contained an engagingly sardonic commentary on the catholicity of his predecessors' interpretations:

> All that I intended at the first was to read those few books which I had in my study upon the Revelation, which I did for my own satisfaction, contention and delight, to see what men did say on that subject. And I did read of some which held Babylon to be the world, the city of the Devil; or the city of wicked men, but all others held it to be Rome, and some would have it to be Heathen Rome, and others Papal. Some have found the revenues of the Popedome, and others the wealth of the King of Spain in the Revelation, and if that were once taken away, the Fall of Babylon would not be long after, which perhaps might give encouragement to Oliver Cromwell to send a navy to Hispaniola to fetch it away. Some have found Gustavus Adolphus, the victorious King of Sweden and the house of Austria there; and to come nearer home some have found our renouned Queen Elizabeth, King James of blessed memory, yea, and men of meaner rank, Mr Burton, Mr Prinne and Dr Bastwicke there, and which I count as senseless as any of the rest, Laodicea, England as they call it; and Philadelphia, Scotland there: and if men will give their minds to mystical interpretation, and believe the common saying, *Quot Verba, Tot Mysteria*, that there be as many mysteries as words in the Revelation, what is it that one may not find there? Some forsake our Church Assemblies, and judge them to be Antichristian, and fetch a warrant for their separation out of the Revelation. . . . Yea, a great in-let to our late civil wars, hath been the misinterpretation of the Revelation. . . .[7]

Hayter pokes fun at the lengths to which interpretation could run, when 'men of meaner rank', like the Puritan martyrs who had their ears cut off in 1637, Burton, Prynne and Bastwick, could

solemnly be claimed for the Apocalypse. The great anti-Puritan
wit, Samuel Butler, made the same point in his *Hudibras*:

> To which it was reveal'd long since
> We were ordain'd by Providence,
> When three Saints' ears, our predecessors,
> The Cause's primitive confessors,
> B'ing crucifyd, the nation stood
> In just so many yeares of blood,
> That, multiplyd by Six, express'd,
> The perfect Number of the Beast,
> And prov'd that we must be the men,
> To bring this work about agen.[8]

But Hayter is going further than Butler: he is arguing that
more than 'men of meaner rank' were to be found in the Book
of Revelation; 'our renouned Queen Elizabeth, King James of
blessed memory' competed for a place there with the 'Cause's
primitive confessors'. Support for Hayter's argument comes from
a surprising quarter. In 1647, when the Roundhead soldiers were
debating the future of England at Putney, Lieutenant-Colonel
Goffe described to his colleagues a dream of the previous night.
From the Book of Revelation – 'that word that we are bid and
commanded to study and look into' – Goffe described his vision
of the downfall of Antichrist. In itself this is not remarkable:
such scenes were commonplace at Putney. What is more important is his remark, in passing, that 'Kings – now, alas, back-
sliders – had once been especially marked out by God as His
Instrument to cast off the Pope's supremacy'.[9]

Before the Reformation, controversialists had been reluctant
to identify even their deadliest enemies with Antichrist.[10] The
Reformers were less inhibited, but the speed with which they
absorbed millenarian language and ideas must not be exaggerated. Luther, in 1522, had been sceptical of the Book of
Revelation as 'neither apostolic nor prophetic' but by 1545 he
had been won to the belief that it *was* an authentic prophecy.
Calvin remained, on the other hand, uninterested in eschatology.
He viewed the Apocalypse with detachment: it had a circumscribed, allegorical significance, and that was all. Calvin remained

wedded to a view of God as, in all significant things, Unknowable. In this, as in so many other respects, he resembled his great
tutor, St Augustine. Augustine, it is true, thought of himself
as living in the Sixth, the last, the old Age of the World. But
his most recent biographer has shown that this inspired in him
a sad stoicism rather than a call to action: 'an attitude that
greatly enhanced the importance of the Catholic Church; it was
already, the Kingdom of God, the Millennium'.[11] Goffe and other
seventeenth-century English Calvinists did not learn chiliasm
from Calvin; in England it was first Wyclif, then Bale and
Bullinger, who developed the idea that the Book of Revelation
foretold the destruction of the Romish Antichrist. But it was John
Foxe who combined this belief with the assumption that the
Christian Emperor had a decisive part to play in the process. It
is this assumption that is echoed ruefully in Goffe's casual remark.

It is also the assumption that will find echoes in countless
pamphlets of the late sixteenth and early seventeenth centuries.
Only recently has the vital significance of John Foxe come to be
recognised. Thanks above all to the pioneering work of Professor Haller, we are coming to recognise an influence on successive generations of English Protestants that goes far beyond
that of a teller of Papist atrocities to credulous bigots. If he were
only that, the mere fact that his volumes, *Acts and Monuments,*
along with the Bible and the works of Bishop Jewel and Erasmus,
were chained in many Tudor churches gives their work a high
value. But Haller convincingly argues higher claims for Foxe:
that he conditioned generations of English Protestants to a belief
in the historic mission of their role; that his influence was decisive upon Milton, and upon countless lesser writers and
preachers, who agitated for a New Jerusalem in the early
forties.[12]

Only up to a point does this argument carry conviction. Foxe's
influence is more ambivalent than this argument allows for. If
it is true that he accustomed generations of Englishmen to the
idea that they were involved in a holy crusade against Antichrist,
he nevertheless believed that salvation would come *through the*

Christian Emperor. The revolutionary implications of the first thesis were checked by the conservative implications of the second thesis. For all its inflammatory language, Foxe's work preaches a conservative message. It is an inspired defence of the *status quo.* Mary Tudor was the agent of Antichrist, but Elizabeth Tudor was the second Constantine.[13] Bishop Bonner was regrettable, but bishops such as Latimer, Cranmer and Ridley were sublime. Whatever else were its effects, a reading of *Acts and Monuments* does not lead logically to belief in a root-and-branch destruction of bishops – or monarchy. And yet Hayter argued that 'a great in-let to our late Civil wars' *was* 'the mis-interpretation of the Revelation'.

Michael Walzer is one recent historian who agrees with Hayter: in his excellent study, *The Revolution of the Saints,* he emphasises the connection between millenarian ideas and political revolution. Not least of the merits of Walzer's study of the origins of radical politics is his refusal to limit himself to the 'fringe sects' and instead to search for his quarry in 'the Puritan mainstream, the true English Calvinists'. But no man in 'the Puritan mainstream' did more to sustain Englishmen in the chiliastic belief that they were destined to crush the Romish Antichrist than John Foxe. Walzer does not mention Foxe once in his index. One sees his dilemma: if Foxe influenced the Revolution of the Saints, why were the Saints so abominably rude about everything that Foxe held dear in 1641?[14] John Jewel, whose defence of the Church of England was another of the four chained books in Tudor churches, is another formative influence on English Protestantism who receives scant attention from Walzer. Walzer speaks of Jewel's homesickness for Zürich when he returns from his Marian exile: 'a kind of spiritual alienation from England'. This is possibly the least useful point to make about Jewel. True, Walzer concedes that Jewel 'made his peace with Elizabeth's system'; hardly an adequate description for the single most powerful and authoritative *apologia* for the Royal Supremacy in sixteenth-century England. And, incidentally, a curious product of 'a kind of spiritual alienation'. The central implausibility in Walzer's work is that he consistently overrates the revolutionary nature of English Calvinism. The revolutionary *potential* was there: Walzer is right that 'a firm basis in radical aspiration and organisation in the seventeenth-century revolution went back to Calvin himself and to the work of the Marian exiles'.[15] But he may be criticised for failing to recognise the extent to which in England (as compared to France and Scotland) this revolutionary potential was held in check by deference to the civil authority. Here the influence of Foxe and Jewel was decisive.

Walzer believed that apocalyptic ideas were linked to the English Revolution, and that they extended beyond the confines of minority sects and had indeed infected 'the Puritan mainstream'. But his argument depended upon omitting Foxe, distorting Jewel. He needed to do neither: all he needed to do was to recognise that – under the tutelage of Foxe and Jewel – millenarian ideas were not, in themselves, a threat to monarchy and episcopacy. They became so only when that tutelage was rejected in 1641. As a preparation for revolution, it was of the utmost importance that Foxe's work conditioned English Protestants to look to the Book of Revelation for salvation. But centrifugal impulses were held in check by Foxe's emphasis on the decisive role to be played by the Christian Emperor and his Church. Yet Foxe's eschatological brinkmanship depended upon a faith in Crown and bishop that became increasingly implausible for many in the reign of Charles I. What happened in 1641 was the rejection of Foxe, *not of the Book of Revelation.* Centrifugal millenarianism replaced centripetal millenarianism.

The next three chapters will attempt to show how far Carlyle's 'Reign of God' – or 'Godly Rule' as I have preferred to call it – influenced the *mainstream* of political thought until the time of the Civil War. What was this 'Godly Rule'? It was a term that might be used by Protestants, or it might not. It was a set of assumptions, not a precise formula for government. Some Protestants in 1603 wanted a Geneva in England; others wanted to preserve, or to modify slightly, the Elizabethan Church; others wanted separate congregations of the faithful. These were differences over means, not over ends. The differences over means

are important and have been studied in depth. Less attention
has been given to the agreement over ends, and yet that too is
important. In the first half of the seventeenth century Carlyle was
right to think that 'men in their several dialects and modes'
were striving nevertheless for the same things. When we look in
the next three chapters at James I as a 'Godly Prince', Archbishop Laud as a 'Godly Bishop', the 'root and branch' ministers
as a 'Godly People', we shall try to emphasise those bonds that
united king, bishop and puritan in the first half of the seventeenth century. The last three chapters will be concerned with
the process by which the idea of a common godly aspiration
ceases to have any relevance for English Protestants in the second
half of the seventeenth century. Carlyle confidently dated this
'Reign of the no-God' from the time that Oliver Cromwell dis-
appears from English history. We shall argue the contrary: that
the man who was 'the last glimpse of the Godlike' in England
struck the most telling of blows against the concept of a 'Godly
Rule'.

1. Thomas Carlyle, *Oliver Cromwell's Letters and Speeches*
(London, Chapman, 1897) I 1.

2. Christopher Hill, *Puritanism and Revolution* (Mercury
Books, 1962) preface.

3. Edmund Gosse, *Father and Son* (Four Square Books,
1959) pp. 56, 57, 58, 188.

4. L. F. Brown, *The Political Activities of the Baptists and
Fifth Monarchy Men in England During the Interregnum* (London, O.U.P.) p. 49.

5. E. Tuveson, *Millennium and Utopia* (Harper Torchbooks,
1964) p. 226.

6. P. Collinson, *The Elizabethan Puritan Movement* (London, Cape, 1967) p. 243.

7. R. Hayter, *A Meaning to the Revelation* (London, 1676)
dedicatory epistle.

8. Samuel Butler, *Hudibras*, III 2 839–848.

9. A. S. P. Woodhouse, ed., *Puritanism and Liberty* (London, Dent, 1951) p. 40.

10. Beryl Smalley, *The Study of the Bible in the Middle Ages* (Oxford, Clarendon Press, 1941) p. 225.

11. Peter Brown, *Augustine of Hippo* (London, Faber, 1967) p. 296.

12. William Haller, *Foxe's* Book of Martyrs *and the Elect Nation* (London, Cape, 1963) *passim*. See also H. J. Cowell, *The Four Chained Books* (London, Kingsgate, 1938); F. A. Yates, 'Queen Elizabeth as Astraea', *Journal of the Warburg and Courtauld Institutes*, x (1947).

13. Perry Miller, *The New England Mind: The Seventeenth Century* (New York, 1939) p. 467, was wrong, therefore, to assert that 'the total eclipse of true Christianity set in for the Puritan historian with Constantine'. The first Christian Emperor provoked a more ambivalent response: admired by Hobbes for his amoral interest in public order (*English Works*, IV 393); by Prynne, on the contrary, for his moral zeal (*Histriomastix* ..., p. 467); only effectively repudiated by Puritans who had shaken off the influence of Foxe. Cf. Roger Williams, *The Bloudy Tenent* ... (London, 1644) p. 95: 'Christianitie fell asleep in Constantine's bosom'; or more drastic still: John Milton, *Selected Prose* (Oxford, 1963) p. 22: 'The Roman Antichrist is merely bred up by Constantine.'

14. This argument is developed in Chapter 4.

15. Michael Walzer, *The Revolution of the Saints* (London, Weidenfeld and Nicolson, 1966) pp. x, 116.

2 Godly Prince

King James I scored a great victory over his puritan subjects at the Hampton Court Conference in 1604: a victory from which he never recovered. The traditional account of events, enshrined in countless textbooks, underlines the fatal lack of touch displayed by the first of the Stuart kings. It is a familiar story. King James – scarred by his experiences with Scottish Presbyterianism – mistook the moderate demands put forward by the English ministers in their Millenary Petition for the theocratic pretensions of a John Knox. He lost his temper with them and warned them that if they did not conform he would 'harry them out of the land'. For both parties 1604 was a turning-point: the English puritans no longer put their trust in a Godly Prince; James, for his part, turned with relief and gratitude to the loving embrace of his bishops. They knew how to treat a prince: no bishop, no king. This version of events has the merit of tidiness. It explains the Anglican belief in Divine Right of Kings, the Puritan faith in Godly Rebellion, Stuart maladroitness – indeed, most of the political happenings of the next forty years are foreshadowed in that dramatic encounter. The only drawback to this version is that it most probably is not true. Dr Curtis has argued convincingly this case.[1] He has shown how many of the seemingly authoritative sources for this version derive from one common, tainted source: the account of the Conference drawn up by William Barlow, bishop of Lincoln. Evidence from other sources has shown that much of what Barlow said was wishful thinking. The Conference was not, as he wished to make out, the high point of harmony between king and bishop. James, as the Christian Emperor, wanted to lay down the pattern of his godly rule, much as his predecessors had done at the start of their reigns. He could see that the English puritan who presented the Millenary Petition was a different animal from the Scottish Presbyterian. He was, therefore, prepared to listen to any request for reforms: the Hampton Court Conference was the logical next step. Its very summoning – irrespective of the decisions taken – was a defeat for Archbishop Bancroft, Barlow and their colleagues. They pleaded that an order that had stood for forty years should be left untouched. To this James had a homely reply:

> It was no reason that because a man had been sick of the poxe 40 years, therefore he should not be cured at length.

As a result of the Conference, many of the reforms for which the puritans had pressed were accepted: most notably the need to counter absenteeism and pluralism. The fate of English puritans was not sealed in a momentary display of petulance. Puritan bitterness dates not from the Conference but from the failure of the bishops subsequently to carry out the reforms that had been agreed upon. Here is the real case against James. He loved the flashy gesture, the display of learning, the histrionics of debate; he was less interested in the more boring business of seeing that orders were carried out. This interpretation has the advantage of making James's ecclesiastical and constitutional failings one: most modern historians would say that James's greatest mistake in his dealings with his parliaments was not in his browbeating of them but in his allowing conciliar influence over them to deteriorate so drastically.[2] In the long run the puritans *were* left with a sense of grievance; this sense of grievance *was* an important factor in the crises that were to follow. But this does not make a revision of the traditional view of the Conference less momentous. At the very lowest, the puritans' grievance is now seen as a more complex and obscure emotion than the traditional simplistic version allowed for. This is something we shall have to explore. But before we do that, we shall have to ask two closely allied questions. First, why should James *want* to lay down a pattern for Godly Rule? Second, why were some of the bishops so anxious to stop such a project from ever getting off the ground, and when it did get off the ground why did they do their very best to misrepresent what had taken place?

James's position is at least more straightforward than that of his bishops. He wanted to lay down a pattern for Godly Rule because he believed in the Divine Right of Kings. More attention is now paid to the limitations of that idea than to its inspiration. The limitations of the idea are worth emphasising, if only because at one time an older generation of historians tended to judge James's reign by his works. In 1603 England faced a phenomenon more rare than a liberal pope: a literate king. James paid dearly for his erudition. When older historians condemned the idea of the Divine Right of Kings – the belief that princes were God's lieutenants on earth – which they found most vigorously asserted in his *The Trew Law of Free Monarchies*, they seemed to be passing judgement on his performance as a king.[3] There are two ways of answering this criticism. First, the limitations of the theory can be stressed: belonging to an age when politics and theology were closely connected and 'all men demanded some form of Divine authority for any theory of Government'; rooted in medieval – and perhaps even earlier – traditions; defensively inspired against the absolute claims of the Papacy. Second, its irrelevance to James's *practice* of kingship can be stressed. He took his Coronation Oath seriously; he operated within the Common Law; he rebuked an over-zealous apologist for royal absolutism in Dr Cowell; he never resorted to imprisonment without trial or the raising of taxes without Parliamentary assent. James only talked – at great length – about practices acceptable to his predecessors on the throne, and indeed to a majority of his subjects. He was the nursing-father of the Church, not Big Brother of the State.

The reaction against the view of James as totalitarian in sympathy may have swung too far. Once we accept that James's writings on kingship are not a blueprint for absolutism, we must still recognise that the very act of making explicit what his predecessor left implicit could (and did) widen divisions between Crown and subject. Why then did he do it? Why did he lecture

Parliament at great length about the limits of their rights, about the nature of his duties? There is an easy answer to this: his vanity, his pedantry, his desire to show off his learning. This is, in part, an explanation of his desire to make speeches; not of the form which they took. His writings and his speeches all reflect one central obsession: the desire to live like a Christian Prince. When James opened Parliament on 19 February 1624, he articulated the obsession more clearly than he ever did before:

> God judge me, I speak as a Christian Prince, never man in a dry and sandy wilderness, where no water is, did thirst more in hot weather for drink, than I do now for a happy conclusion of this parliament.[4]

A 'Christian Prince' was no cant phrase, idly chosen. In his *Basilikon Doron* (1599) he had argued the need for kings, above all others, to study Scripture closely to understand why 'godly Kings' should rule over 'the people of God'. In his *The Trew Law of Free Monarchies* (1598) he made clear the order of priorities as sources for understanding kingship: first the Bible; then the laws of the land; then the laws of Nature. In his introduction to *An Apologie for the Oath of Allegiance* (1609), James devoted much labour and ingenuity to teasing out from the Book of Revelation the conclusion that Rome was Antichrist: the enemy of the Godly Prince.

James was not unique in this obsession; only in his ability *as a monarch* to make articulate the obsession. It was an obsession which he shared with the majority of his Protestant subjects. They too found in Scripture – and especially in the Book of Revelation – comfort for the view that they were locked in a struggle with Antichrist at Rome. We are perhaps too ready to identify millenarianism with the 'lunatic fringe' groups that multiplied in the Civil War and Commonwealth period. The association of millenarianism with radical dissent was most powerfully argued in the work of Professor Norman Cohn, *The Pursuit of The Millennium*. But it is a mistake to identify the Book of Revelation *exclusively* with the dottiest sects, who embraced it most fervently. Perhaps the construction of Professor Cohn's book lends itself to misinterpretation. We jump from the 'Messianic reign of John of Leyden' in the sixteenth century to an appendix which deals in detail with the Ranters in mid-seventeenth-century England.[5] This is not a chronological progression: early-seventeenth-century England is omitted. But it is not a logical progression either. Professor Cohn quite properly emphasised the inspiration of the Book of Revelation to the socially underprivileged – quite properly, since it was this aspect of its influence that was germane to his thesis. He showed how the messianic expectations which it aroused influenced the rootless and this was why, once the Roman Catholic Church had become powerful and centralised, it abolished texts that encouraged hopes of an Earthly Paradise. And this was why, as early as A.D. 431, the Council of Ephesus had condemned belief in the Millennium as a superstitious aberration. But Professor Cohn never argued that this was the *only* effect that the Book of Revelation had. Indeed, in his introduction he drew attention to a *centripetal* as well as to a *centrifugal* effect.

In medieval Europe, from the fourth century onwards, men had been encouraged to expect a mighty Emperor to arise to avenge the slaying of the Christians by the Ishmaelites. This so-called Sibylline eschatology had enormous influence throughout the Middle Ages. When printing was invented, prophecies about the Emperor of the Last Days were among the first books to appear. No ruling monarch needed to fear the Book of Revelation if some sharp-witted interpreter of Scripture were to identify *him* with such an Emperor. James I had no such fears.

It is easy to forget how very respectable the Book of Revelation had become in England in the early years of the seventeenth century. Contemporaries forgot too. Thus Richard Baxter could write to a friend in 1657 – with all the Ranter excesses before his eyes – and complain testily: 'I deny not the Apocalypse to be intelligible, but it followeth not that you or I understand it.' And a friend congratulated him: 'You say well that we lay not our opposition to Popery chiefly on the dark Revelation prophesy, or on the question who is the Antichrist.' But Baxter admitted that when he was younger such speculations had fired his imagination – 'My juvenile fancye being more daring' was his prim apology.[6]

Old men forget. At least they inflate the misdeeds of their youth. None more so than Baxter, who has elsewhere related – in loving (tedious) detail – his failings as a child.[7] The truth was that *before* the Civil War no great daring was needed to pin one's hopes for salvation on the prophecies in Revelation. One man had made the pursuit of the Millennium respectable and orthodox. The man who domesticated the Apocalypse was John Foxe.

Foxe is often called a great writer, but for the wrong reasons. The work on which his fame rests, *Acts and Monuments,* is usually called *The Book of Martyrs.* This is a significant slip. If we see Foxe primarily as the great chronicler of the sufferings of the Protestant martyrs in Mary's reign, contemporaries saw him differently: as the man *who gave meaning* to these sufferings. Foxe believed that a divine pattern could be discerned in history. There were five periods in Church history. He was writing in the fifth period. From where did Foxe derive his five periods? From the Book of Revelation. When Foxe had synthesised the old Sibylline eschatology with a detailed account of the sufferings of the Marian martyrs, he had created a masterpiece. It was the harrowing descriptions of the martyrdoms that gave the book its emotive appeal; it was the underlying philosophy that canalised these emotions. Without this philosophy, Foxe would have written a compelling tract against Rome; and nothing more. The philosophy made it the indispensable apology for the role of the Christian Emperor.

Foxe argued from the Book of Revelation that there were five periods of Church history. The first three hundred years after Christ were the time of Church purity and persecution by the heathen emperors. The next three hundred years were the time of the Christian Empire; the Emperor Constantine ushered in a golden period of peace. The influence of Rome retarded the Church from A.D. 600 until the Norman Conquest. Nevertheless, these first three periods represented a thousand years of comparative stability. But the accession of Hildebrand marked the beginning of the reign of Antichrist. Satan was let loose when the Papacy took over the powers of the Christian Emperor. Foxe was writing at the time of the fifth period, of the struggle between Christ and Antichrist. For this was the significance of the English Reformation: it marked the triumphant return of the Christian Emperor. This had been indeed the great rationalisation offered in the preamble to the Act in Restraint of Appeals of 1533:

> Where by divers sundry old authentic histories and chronicles it is manifestly declared and expressed that this realm of England is an empire, and so hath been accepted in the world, governed by one Supreme Head and King having the dignity and royal estate of the imperial crown.

Almost all the great Anglican apologists in the sixteenth century – John Jewel, William Tyndale, Edward Grindal, John Bale and James Pilkington among others – make this passage the foundation of their claims for the Church of England.[8] Foxe was their necessary complement. He showed that the Marian persecutions represented the response of Antichrist to the imperial challenge. When things were at their lowest, in answer to Latimer's prayers, there had arisen the second Constantine:

> ... at the change whereof Queen Elizabeth was appointed and anointed, for whome this grey-headed father so earnestly prayed in his imprisonment: Through whose true, natural and imperial crowne, the brightnesse of God's word was set up again to confound the dark and false-vizored Kingdom of Antichrist.[9]

Foxe's *Acts and Monuments* and Jewel's *The Defence of the Apology of the Church of England* were often chained in Tudor churches along with the Bible and Erasmus's *Paraphrases*. As late as 1629 William Prynne in his pamphlet, *Anti-Arminianisme* ..., underlined the importance of this fact when he made reference to: 'Queen Elizabeth's pious Raigne ... that incomparable ornament of our English Church, Mr. John Jewell, Bishop of Salisbury ... laborious Mr. John Foxe ... his renowned Booke of Martyrs (which every Archbishop, Deane, and Arch-Deacon in the Kingdome were enjoyned to buy, and to place in their Halls, or great Chambers, that they might serve for the use of their servants and of strangers, by the expresse Ecclesiastical Canons, published by Queen Elizabeth's authority with the assent of her Clergy ... 1571).'[10] The resolution that Prynne mentioned was never totally enforced, although the advice contained in it was widely followed. What is of interest is to see its consequences: when a Nonconformist as late as 1629 can speak of Foxe, Jewel and the reign of Elizabeth with such veneration. Much of the argument between Anglican and Nonconformist in the reign of James I revolves round interpretations of Foxe. How godly *was* the rule of Elizabeth? Foxe's history encouraged a reverent approach to Elizabeth: she was the culmination of history; the retort of God to the challenge of Rome. Anglicans could therefore support the *status quo* in James I's reign by direct reference to Foxe and Jewel. To this Nonconformists, who were also under the spell of Foxe, had two replies. First, Foxe did not mean that everything in the Elizabethan Church was perfect; there was room for further reforms. Second, even if the Elizabethan Church *were* perfect, there had been a decline in the reign of her successor. The most damaging charge that Prynne can make against bishops like Laud is that they were deviating from the principles of the Elizabethan Church. It is this which lends an air of unreality to some of the debates in the reigns of James I and Charles I: Anglicans and Nonconformists were fussing about who was more faithful to the traditions of Foxe and Jewel. This air of unreality exasperated the Presbyterian Scot, Robert Baillie, who felt that there was more to Godly Rule than a purified Elizabethan Church. But there were Anglicans too who did not wish to rest their case on Foxe and Jewel.

It is at this point that an attempt must be made to understand the mentality of those who would not rest content with a 'Foxe-ier-than-thou attitude'. There was a very good reason why, in the last years of Elizabeth's reign, bishops such as Barlow and Bancroft should view with misgivings the emphasis that Foxe gave to the dynamic role of the Christian Emperor. Elizabeth's successor was likely to be James: a man interested in theology, and educated by Scottish Presbyterians. Even in the year of the Armada, some bishops were becoming more exercised

at the thought of James than at that of Philip. This alarm provoked the famous sermon of 1588 by Bancroft, when he put
forward the argument – so audacious in the age of Foxe – that
episcopacy did not depend on the support of the civil magistrate.[11] It existed, *iure divino*, by the grace of God, not *iure
humano*, by the favour of the King. After James came to the
throne, Bancroft's thesis was developed by broodingly vigilant
colleagues such as William Barlow, George Carleton and Thomas
Sparke.

George Carleton's *Jurisdiction, Regall, Episcopall, Papall* is
one of the key works of a development in Anglican apologetics
that has never quite received its proper attention. In the dedicatory epistle to this work, he stressed its novelty: that it
represented a shift in Anglican thinking from the question of
supremacy to the question of jurisdiction. Hitherto, slipshod
workmen had mingled together the jurisdiction of Church and
king: his task was 'to distinguish this confused masse, and to
give to each his own right'. The task was particularly difficult
because 'none of later yeares hath troden this path before me,
whose footsteps might have directed me'. Against Papal claims,
the Tudor apologists for the Church had necessarily to deal with
supremacy, not jurisdiction. Carleton declared that he did not
wish to diminish the royal powers (a point unceasingly echoed by
all his colleagues), but the Tudor solution was a solution only
of the question of supremacy, not of jurisdiction:

> Stephen Gardiner . . . had found this massie crowne of
> jurisdiction upon the Pope's head, so he took it with gold,
> silver, copper, drosse and all: and set it upon the King's head.

Carleton claims that the Papists have encroached in two directions: upon King and upon Church. Against the Papal subordination of temporal to spiritual, Carleton can join the Tudor bishops
in a robust defence of the Royal Supremacy in external jurisdiction. But to this he adds an important rider: 'all spirituall
power to the Church'. This distinction between the two spheres is
based on the difference between *execution* (which belongs to the
king) and *interpretation* (which belongs to the priest). Within
the province of the Church are: examination of controversies of

faith; judgement of heretics; excommunication of offenders; ordination of priests and deacons. Of these, he says:

> We confesse that in this power the prince hath no part, and that Bishops and pastors have this power onely, from the divine ordinance, and not from earthly princes.

The prince's role in ecclesiastical matters is limited to execution. In that capacity, can there be an appeal to him from the interpretation of an 'Ecclesiastical Judge'? Carleton concedes the right of appeal to Caesar, but then drastically limits the scope of the concession:

> We answere, Saint Paul had no meaning to make Caesar judge of any point of faith. But whereas he was persecuted by the high Priests, who sought his life, in this matter of coactive power Saint Paul giveth jurisdiction to Caesar.

If the king commands preachers to do their duty and punishes them for neglect of duty, he is acting legitimately but this is no symbol of spiritual jurisdiction. For in matters such as preaching the king has no part except that of execution, which is outside the sphere of jurisdiction. But the converse to this is that if the magistrate should neglect his duties or command false doctrine to be preached:

> in this case, the Church hath warrant to maintaine the truth.

Carleton makes clear the implications of this position:

> For the preservation of true doctrine in the Church, the Bishops are the great watch-men. Herein they are authorised by God. If Princes withstand them in these things, they have warrant not to obey Princes, because with these things Christ hath put them in trust.

Whatever Carleton might say to the contrary, the effect of such teaching was to diminish the royal authority. He calls princes gods, it is true, but in the same way that Hitler called Ribbentrop a second Bismarck: the praise stated was less than the self-praise implied. And indeed in the very act of calling princes gods, Carleton emphasises the superiority of the priest:

> We find then that the Prince is called a God in respect of the

Priest, but we can never find that the Priest is called a God in respect of the Prince.

In a similar manner, Carleton argues that external coactive jurisdiction was not left by Christ to the Church for the first three hundred years of the Church's existence so that it was 'without Princes for her nourcing Fathers that by wanting it so long, we might understand the greatnesse of the blessing'. So princes are a great blessing: Carleton seems here to lean towards Foxe. But a few lines later we are reminded how dispensable they are. For how did the Church fare without a Constantine? Carleton shows that it did not do at all badly:

> For by this spirituall power without coaction, the Church was called, faith was planted, divils were subdued, the nations were taken out of the power of darknesse, the world was reduced to the obedience of Christ.

How far Carleton has moved from Foxe! The Emperor Constantine, the climax of Foxe's history, becomes a shabby epilogue to Carleton's account. In the remainder of his pamphlet Carleton is at pains to dissociate his position from that of the Papist. The Papist lays claim to coactive, as well as to spiritual, jurisdiction; in so doing he blurs the distinction between Church and State to the detriment of the State, as equally do the Foxes and Jewels to the detriment of the Church. The Pope's claim to use only spiritual censures is cant. The power to excommunicate and depose rulers, to release subjects from allegiance to the civil magistrate: these are claims to a coactive power and, as such, are intrusions upon the royal authority. In seeking to define the boundaries of Church and State, Carleton can thus pose as the defender of the king's interests as well as of the Church's; yet the limiting of royal authority to external matters implied the subordination of State to Church.[12]

George Downame made clear that he accepted the logic of this argument.[13] In one sermon he drew a direct comparison between the status of bishop and of king:

> Than which, what Authority is more glorious upon the Earth? the Magistrates indeed having the Keys of an earthly Kingdome, have also power to loose and to bind the Bodies of

their Subjects and to commit the same to a Jaylor or Execu-
tioner, but the Ministers having the Keys of the Kingdom of
Heaven, have power to bind and loose the Soul of Men?

His argument is built on etymology: on the link between
Honos and *Onos*. The extent of the honour must correspond to
the extent of the burden. But men lay the greatest burden upon
the Ministers: the charge of their immortal souls. Therefore 'they
must be fain to ascribe unto them the greatest Honour'. He
argues from patristic authorities that:

> Ministers excel Princes, as far as Gold is better than Lead,
> as Heaven surpasseth the Earth, as the Soul excelleth the Body.

The Papists err in inferring from such maxims clerical superiority in external authority; moreover, they apply these attributes
to their Lord God, the Pope, not simply to the ministry. They
would, he acknowledges, have a sound case if they thought in
terms of spiritual excellency and of the Church. Yet loyalty to
the Crown should restrain a subject from making a comparison
between the power of Church and king; a comparison which, as
he had demonstrated, could only be unflattering to the king.
Despite this, he concludes with a thrilling assertion of clerical
superiority:

> it cannot be denied, but those whom the Lord calleth to the
> Ministry, he advanceth above the condition of other Men
> ... which might seem to become Angels rather than Men ...[14]

Another Jacobean divine, Thomas Sparke, asserted the *iure
divino* claim for episcopacy, and denied that it struck at the
Crown.[15] William Barlow pointed out that, while it was natural
for kings to be jealous of their thrones, the jealousy of Pilate had
destroyed Christ. God is wary of giving too much power to
kings. He quoted from Scripture: 'Be wise, O Kings, lest you
lose the right way to Heaven.' God never intended that the support of the Church should rest upon royal caprice:

> ... for that had beene the way to make them not nourishing
> Fathers, but either pinching suppressors, or at best colde and
> wary favorers of the same ...

Kings should not be afraid of bishops. They will not encroach upon the Royal Supremacy, as Papists do. Or, more truly, if they do encroach it will be in a less exceptionable manner. The difference is not in the intrinsic nature of the authority but in the ostentatious way that the execution of that authority is carried out: the bishops of the Church of England, unlike the Papists, work 'by meanes weak in shew, mightie in effect'. This is to go even further than Carleton had done in asserting the autonomy of the Church. Barlow argues that 'those fetters made to bind Kings are Documents of Faith . . . not Thunderers of disturbances'. Opponents could argue that they remained fetters none the less. Bishops are not troublemakers. Here, for Barlow, they diverge crucially from Papists:

> Bishops and Priests use the Keyes committed to them, towards their Sovereigns for winning their soules, not for disturbing their states; for preaching to them, not factioning against them.

But, if this superior power of preaching is threatened, Barlow's answer is substantially the same as Carleton's: resistance by the watchmen. Moreover, the sovereign whose soul has been won over retains precious little freedom of action. The Catholic apologist, Parsons, had cited countries such as Poland, Hungary and Bohemia to support his plea for toleration. Barlow dismissed such arguments as irrelevant to the English monarchy, where policies are determined not by the precedents of men but by the precepts of God, working through His Church:

> He knowes what Princes ought to doe, not regarding what they please to doe, being desirous to governe by Christian pietie than Irreligious Policie . . .[16]

The theories of this group of Church of England divines taken together constitute a formidable challenge to Tudor Anglican thought. It must be emphasised that these were not *obiter dicta* of one or two bishops, scattered among orthodox pronouncements. They were carefully-thought-out arguments to the Tudor orthodoxies of Foxe and Jewel. The titles of some of their works are themselves illuminating: *Jurisdiction, Regall, Episcopall and Papall* by Carleton; *A Sermon Defending the Honourable Function of Bishops* by Downame (this at the consecration of Mountague as bishop of Bath and Wells); *Concerning the Antiquitie and Superioritie of Bishops,* by Barlow. The dates of these works are significant too: 1610, 1608 and 1606 respectively. In other words, Hampton Court had not resolved the Anglican doubts about James that had originally prompted Bancroft's sermon of 1588, any more than it had dashed the Puritan hopes for reform through the civil magistrate. In the skill with which Barlow obscures both these uncomfortable truths in his official account of the Conference a finesse, amounting almost to genius, is displayed. We had seen something of Barlow's subtlety, in another sermon, when he praised James for his severity against a Roman Catholic polemicist. Or rather, he praised him for the form which that severity took. He praised James for considering the rope as the most suitable answer to such men and for his magnanimity in forbearing from laying his opponents low with his matchless learning:

> ... And with all humblenesse I could hartely wish that Your Highness could be pleased, from henceforth, to contemne the rest, as Him, and not to goe forth any more unto these Battails (they will glorie in it though they be sure to receive the foile).

A marginal note on the pamphlet, in a contemporary hand, underlines the point: 'good counsell to a King'.[17] The words might be taken as the theme of this movement: kings are to be revered, but only if they act upon the assumption that the reverence means nothing. Above all, let them not think that they can take over the bishops' role of watchmen!

These bishops might be sceptical about Foxe's vision of a Godly Prince, but they were not sceptical about his vision of a Godly Rule. They shared Foxe's belief that English Protestants were fighting a critical battle in the last stages of history with Antichrist. If they believed, unlike Foxe, that salvation would come through no reincarnated Emperor Constantine but through the unremitting vigilance of England's watchmen-bishops, they at least agreed with Foxe about the nature of their adversary.

This was how George Downame described the Roman Church:

> The Church of Rome is the whore of Babylon, the see of
> Antichrist, the mother of all fornications and abominations,
> being also embrued, and as it were dyed red with the blood of
> the Saints, and of the Martyrs of Jesus.[18]

Clergymen with this apocalyptic vision were unpersuaded
that their salvation could be left in the hands of a Godly Prince.
Barlow's great achievement was to translate the watchful para-
noia of the Hampton Court Conference into the myth of loving
harmony between Church and Crown. Later the myth claimed
the man. James I became a better churchman than his Barlows
and Bancrofts could ever have dared to hope. But this was a long
process, and so was Puritan disenchantment with the civil magistrate. This truth has been obscured by the propagandist success
of Barlow's account, and its consequence has been to make Puritan political thought in the period after the Hampton Court Conference seem tawdry and somehow irrelevant. All those loving
professions of regard for the civil magistrate, the hymns of
praise to Emperor Constantine and to Queen Elizabeth, those
near-blasphemous analogies of kings with gods – what more are
they than the desperate strivings of a persecuted minority after
respectability? After Barlow, the English Puritan seems for ever
frozen in the defensive posture of the whipped cur at the feet
of its royal master.

But if we can rid ourselves of this image we may be in a position to do greater justice to the political thought of the early
Jacobean Puritans. The early seventeenth century is now – thanks
to the work of scholars such as Dr Collinson and Mr Christopher Hill[19] – recognised as a crucial formative period in the
development of Puritan casuistry, social and economic attitudes,
and organisation. The previous neglect of these features of a
period sandwiched between the more glamorous convulsions of
the Elizabethan era – the polemics of Cartwright and Travers,
the attempt by Field to set up in England a classical structure of
organisation on the lines of Geneva, the scurrility of the Marprelate Tracts – that preceded it and the open 'root and branch'
agitation that followed it: this has now been handsomely re-

dressed. But the Puritan political thought of this period still receives less attention that it should. And yet for the rest of the century it is not merely for their casuistry that English Puritans will go on invoking the name of figures such as Bolton, Preston, Sibbes and Reynolds.[20] They will return – and this is equally as evident in the letters as in the pamphlets of the later period – to these earlier masters in the belief that they have something relevant to say to them about the authority of the civil magistrate. And, in invoking them, they will do so with the assurance that they, too, are part of an older tradition still, going back to Tudor times and to the writings of Foxe and Jewel. In a notable attack on the bishops' *iure divino* claims for their office, Richard Baxter in 1659 made precisely that point:

> If you have read the writings of Jewell, Pilkington, Alley, Ussher, Hall, Davenant, etc., with such like on one side and the writings of the New Episcopal Divines that are most followed on the other side, I need not tell you the difference.[21]

And when Baxter wrote to Eliot in 1671 on the merits of non-separation, he extolled the saintliness of men such as 'Sibs, Preston, Bolton'. In another letter of 1673 he told an Anglican that his spiritual ancestors were men such as Baynes, Reynolds and Foxe.[22] We shall see in a later chapter how, in the crucial controversy of the Interregnum about the admission of communicants to the Lord's Supper, time and time again controversialists appeal to the traditions of 'old nonconformity'. Because these traditions were imprecise – so imprecise that *opponents* on this issue such as Baxter and Prynne could invoke them with equal sincerity – the inference must not be drawn that they were, therefore, meaningless. Prynne, John Humfrey and John Timson were probably the three most important controversialists in the Interregnum who argued against clerical claims to suspend the ungodly from the Sacrament of the Lord's Supper. They saw themselves, very self-consciously, in the lineage of Jacobean Puritanism. It is interesting that Humfrey should offer in defence of Timson that 'he was, it seems, bred up under the famous Robert Bolton, and so one of the old Puritans . . . deeply affected

... with the evil of the neglect in many places of the Sacrament'.[23] There is the same feeling, as with Baxter, of identity with those who defended the *Tudor* Church of England rather than with those who attacked it. Our most recent historian of Elizabethan Puritanism has reminded us that even Field's organisation of English Presbyterian *classes* in the 1580s was 'a world of half-loaves and make-believe'[24] – and this is commonly regarded as the high point of English Presbyterianism – but it was still too clericalist, too close to Geneva, for the appetite of the Jacobean Puritans. In the dispute between Archbishop Whitgift and Thomas Cartwright, the sympathies of the seventeenth-century Puritan, William Prynne, were not with his sixteenth-century Puritan predecessor. Indeed, Prynne did not see Cartwright as his predecessor at all: Jewel and Foxe were his great mentors. He was even tactless enough to refer quite brutally to Cartwright in controversy as an 'opposite'. This drew a stinging rebuke from George Gillespie, the champion of Scottish Presbyterianism:

> And are the old non-Conformists of blessed memory, now Opposites? Where are we? I confesse as he stands affected, he is opposite to the old non-Conformists, and they to him.[25]

Such was the charm of Prynne: a man who approached controversies with an ever open mouth. And he was right, not Gillespie. If English Puritans had followed the trail of Cartwright the whole course of religious history in the seventeenth century might have been profoundly different. To the chagrin of the Presbyterian Scots they did not; the one outstanding exception was Alexander Leighton.[26] Most English Puritans would have agreed with Prynne in rejecting Cartwright as a founder of English nonconformity. As Baxter put it:

> The nonconformists now are not the same that lived in the daies of our forefathers, nor are obliged by that name to defend their positions.[27]

The Jacobean Nonconformists disliked the emphasis that Tudor Presbyterians, such as Cartwright, gave to clerical power and to the downgrading of the civil magistrate. They responded by affirming the great truths laid down by Foxe and Jewel. And they saw that these truths now faced a twin challenge: from the *iure divino* claims for *episcopacy*, no less than for *Presbyterianism*. This was the menace posed by the writings of the new Church of England apologists, such as Downame, Barlow, Bancroft and Bilson.[28] A critic of Downame noted of his *iure divino* claim of episcopacy:

> ... It is a doctrine contrarying the doctrine of the Church of England, professed even by the Bishops themselves (Jewell and Whitgift) till of late dayes: when as men wearie to holde any longer *in Capite* and of the King: they begin to change their tenure into socage and designed to be free even from Knights Service.

This anonymous Puritan drew attention to the similarity of the views expressed by both Downame and Barlow, and asked why 'our Lord Bishops' were no longer content with authority from the civil magistrate, but they must needs 'enjoy it now by a new found pattent even *iure divino*?'[29] Another critic (probably Reynolds, the leading Puritan at Hampton Court) argued that the Barlows and Downames 'have contrarie to the judgement of all protestant writers upon this place ... fancied to themselves another sort of Bishops'. Their new emphasis on the priestly character of the ministry ran contrary to Anglican tradition, as maintained by Whitaker, 'the David against the Popish Goliath', Bullinger, Alley, Nowell, Fulke and 'that worthy Jewell', which defended episcopacy as convenient and lawful, not as of direct divine appointment.[30] Paul Baynes was one Puritan who saw the humbug in Carleton's suggestion that bishops required a nursing-father when they had done so very well for three hundred years without one:

> And it is absurd to think that those who were fit to gather a church and bring it to fitnesse from small beginnings should not be fit to governe it but stand in need to have some one sent who might rule them and the churches they had collected.[31]

Baynes saw correctly that these writers had made a Godly Prince redundant. In the same year that Baynes attacked *iure divino* Anglicanism a Catholic controversialist could make play on the Anglican schism: some Anglicans derived authority from 'letters Patentes of their Prince, and general consent of the Parliament house, as many English Protestants did in the days of King Edward, and at the beginning of Queene Elizabeths raygne. But now their new Attorneys . . . lay clayme to the pedigree of our Bishops'.[32] 1621 – the year in which the 'New Attorneys' were evident – was the year in which Prynne graduated from Oxford University and entered Lincoln's Inn. In 1622 John Preston became lecturer at Lincoln's Inn. Two hostile critics, Anthony Wood and Peter Heylyn, suggested that Preston taught Prynne to be a radical.[33] There is no substantial evidence to support their suggestion of an intimate understanding between the two; if there was, however, a different inference might be drawn. Preston's influence at Court, through the Duke of Buckingham, albeit transient, could underline once more the hope for Puritans that reform within the Church could be won via the Crown, in the same way that this prospect terrified at the time some Laudian bishops.[34] Hampton Court had not destroyed the Puritan faith in a Godly Prince.

To Puritans, therefore, the defence of the Christian Emperor was more than a polite gesture. It was a central tenet of their faith. Brought up on the pages of Foxe, they responded with gratitude to the Christian Emperor who could deliver them from Antichrist. No doubt Prynne exaggerated when he defined Puritans simply as 'those who maintaine the Kings Ecclesiasticall Prerogative',[35] but something of this feeling touched them all. It touched William Bradshaw, arguing that the mark of the Puritan was a defence of episcopacy, *iure humano*. It touched the anonymous pamphleteer who invited James I, as a Christian Emperor, to call a general Council against the usurping power of the Pope. It touched Robert Bolton, when he defended in 1621 'that Imperiall Majesty, which is originally and individually inherent in the person of a Monarchicall Soveraigne', and extolled Queen Elizabeth in these words:

Of sweetest and dearest memory, the happiest instrument of God's glory of her sexe, since the most blessed Virgine, I say, since she rose into the Imperiall throne, what a deale of glory and light, admiration and honour, what missiles of unparallelled deliverinces and preservations, have crowned this famous land.[36]

Bolton is linked with Prynne in an interesting way. Bolton had been the tutor at Brasenose College, Oxford, of Edmund Bagshaw, a lawyer from the Middle Temple. In 1635 Bagshaw printed these sermons of Bolton, with an enthusiastic introduction. In 1639 Bagshaw delivered two discourses with the common theme that Parliament could be held without bishops, and that bishops should not meddle in civil affairs. In 1640 Henry Burton bracketed the sufferings of himself, Bastwick and Prynne together with the suspension of Bagshaw as evidence of the common hostility to *iure divino* Laudianism:

... was not a Learned Reader in the Law of the Temple, now a member of the Parliament, inhibited and suspended from his Reading, because he undertook to prove, that Prelaticall Jurisdiction was not *Iure Divino,* by Divine Authority?[37]

Burton was right that the three Puritan martyrs of 1637 claimed, as did Bagshaw, that their hostility to bishops was limited to those who were dethroning the Godly Prince. But of these three, probably only Prynne shared with Bagshaw and Bolton the Jacobean concern for the powers of the civil magistrate. For Burton, already inclining to congregationalism, and Bastwick, already inclining to Presbyterianism, a defence of *iure humano* episcopacy was simply a useful stick with which to beat the Laudians.

Burton and Bastwick were probably somewhat precocious among English Puritans in entering into their commitments before 1641. But already by the late 1630s the Jacobean Puritan cult of the Godly Prince was wearing thin. Bishops like Barlow and Downame had rebelled against the tyranny of Foxe because they resented so much dependence on the civil magistrate. Were there no kindred critics among English Puritans – apart from those who accepted, like Bastwick did, a Presbyterian clericalist solution? We have seen how psychologically dependent the English

Puritan was on the Christian Prince. This is true even of the Baptists.

In the reign of James I, even those who went further than Nonconformists were prepared to do, and who urged separation from an impure Church, were affected by centripetal millenarianism. A Baptist, Leonard Busher, writing in favour of toleration in 1614, invoked the figure of Constantine:

> I read that Constantine the Emperor, called the great, wrote to the bishop of Rome, that he would not force and constrain any man to the faith, but only admonish, and commit the judgment to God.

More striking is his acceptance of the need for the unity of Jerusalem. With an ingenious twist, he turns the stock argument of opponents against themselves. Granted that one desires uniformity, persecution is not the way of achieving it; instead, it will make the Church but 'a confused Babel'. From the Book of Revelation, Busher warns of the danger that the king might delegate authority to the Beast, and argues for decisive action from the Christian Prince:

> And the Scripture saith, the ten horns, by which I understand ten Kings, shall hate the whore and make her desolate and naked.... Therefore believing Kings may safely walk in the steps of their father Abraham, and with their swords defend their subjects against their adversaries.

Busher's final plea is not for restraint from the magistrate, but for the full use of his power 'against the bloody persecution of antichrist and all his bloody bishops and ministers, and so become nursing fathers unto the church of Christ'.[38]

In others words Busher – the Baptist pleading for toleration – accepts the basic premises of a 'Godly Rule'. One important difference between his and Foxe's interpretation of Revelation is that Antichrist is identified with the bishops. In Foxe's history the bishops are the ally of the Crown against the Papacy, which is Antichrist. But even Foxe's disciple, Prynne, was to modify this view to accommodate the phenomenon of Laudianism. Prynne treated Laud and those associated with him as disguised Papists, and extended the label of 'Antichrist' to include them.

But, until 1641, he accepted the distinction between the 'Laudian' wing of the Church and the 'good' bishops, who were perpetuating the Foxeian tradition of war against Antichrist.[39] No such distinction was made by Busher: this is the difference between separatism and nonconformity. Yet Busher, as much as Foxe and Prynne, accepts the need for strong action from the Christian Prince.

The idea of what life would be like without a 'Godly Rule' is nowhere more graphically expressed than in the 1621 sermon of the Puritan, Robert Bolton:

> Take Soveraignty from the face of the earth, and you turne it into a Cockpit. Men would become cut-throats and cannibals one unto another. Murder, adulteries, incests, rapes, robberies, perjuries, witchcrafts, blasphemies, all kinds of villanies, outrages, and savage cruelty, would overflow all Countries. We should have a very hell upon earth, and the face of it covered with blood, as it was once with water.[40]

Did Hobbes put it more terrifyingly than that? And we have seen too how the distance between James and his English Puritan subjects had been exaggerated for their own purposes by some bishops at the start of his reign. Even so, that distance had widened during his reign: an aftermath of the failure to implement the Hampton Court proposals. Surely English Puritans too had misgivings about such a dependence on the civil magistrate – especially if they sympathised with the complaints of the Commons against, for instance, James's foreign policy and his dispensations to Papists? Some did, and began to cast doubts on Foxe's exaltation of the Godly Prince. There were not enough of them to satisfy Scottish Presbyterians, such as Robert Baillie, who wanted an end to the cult of Elizabeth. And even those who did escape from the tutelage of Foxe disgusted men like Baillie by continuing to accept Foxe's belief that the key to Godly Rule lay in the Book of Revelation. They questioned not his methods of search but the conclusions that he drew from it. The leader in this field was Thomas Brightman.

Brightman published his *A Revelation of the Revelation* in 1615. His critique of Foxe bites deeper than Busher's, because it strikes at the indispensability of the civil magistrate as well as of the bishops. Brightman was polite to 'our John Foxe' as well he might: he was the pioneer in the field of apocalyptic interpretation. But Brightman stressed Foxe's limitations:

> Somewhat more general and more obscure, such as the condition of that time would suffer, but this is most full and copious, because there was nowe greater knowledge of matters attained than ever before this.

Foxe's account had ended in 1560. Brightman argued the need to supplement this with the insight gained from the achievement of Elizabeth's reign.

From his reading of Revelation, Brightman drew a picture not unlike that of Bolton's:

> For now is the last Act begun of a most long and dolefull tragedy, which shall wholly overflow with scourges, slaughters, destructions.

What is missing in Brightman's account is Bolton's assurance that salvation will come through the civil magistrate. He makes the obligatory eulogy of Elizabeth – ' so excelling in all things that are praiseworthy, as the like to her no age ever saw' – but his heart is patently not in it. He notes the 'dissolutnes and licentiousness in the lyves of all men'; how much enjoyed in the reign of Elizabeth were the jests of that virulent enemy of bishops, Martin Marprelate, among the common people; and warns that God's favour will depart from England 'unless we meet him speedily with fruits worthy of true repentance, and of his glorious Gospell'.

For Brightman believed, *pace* Foxe, that the *decline* of the Church dated from Constantine, the first Christian Emperor. In one passage, he referred to 'men called Christian Princes, but they exercised the savage cruelty of the Heathen under that name'. And although the accession of Elizabeth had caused the trumpet to be blown, the parallel with Constantine was a warning against too great a reliance upon her – or upon her learned successor:

> But nowe is his Kingdome to be especially extolled with

praises, when he doth make his Majesty to be visible after a sort in the Kings themselves.... And yet this is no strange thing either. He raigned thus in auncient times by means of Constantine, and other Godly Emperours.

It was not politic to attack Elizabeth directly, but she could be wounded by analogy. Foxe had compared her to Constantine; Brightman would make the analogy tell against her. What had Constantine achieved? Christians were set free; more remarkable still, they had an Emperor of their faith – 'which never before came into the thought of any man, no not in a dream'. But the time of rejoicing was short: 'but halfe an hour long'. There were outward trappings of virtue, 'yet as touching true piety, all began to waxe worse and worse'. Christianity was 'now more corrupted through outward love and happiness, then it was when the cruel enemies sword was hacking upon the necks and backs of Christians'.

Brightman argued against expecting too much from a Godly Prince. It was precisely at the point 'in the midst of such a glorious peace and in the time of so great a desire to advance the Christian profession' that 'for true Christians is the time for the setting and going apart'. It was when Constantine came to the throne that 'the Church begins to hide it selfe in secret, by departing aside from the view of the world into a certain secret sanctuary'. The Godly Ruler frustrates, not advances, Godly Rule; only by separating into secret conclaves can 'anything intire sincere and sound' be preserved.[41]

During the Civil War both Presbyterians and Independents would appeal to the writings of Thomas Brightman. Now while it is true that he identified the Reformed Church of Scotland with Philadelphia – and the Church of England with Laodicea – he says little in detail about Presbyterian discipline. And ultimately Presbyterians such as Baillie recognised that his influence was inimical to their hopes: that his reading of Revelation encouraged most those who wished to see the establishment of separate congregations. Brightman was not the first apologist for congregationalism, nor was he the most profound commentator on the Apocalypse. But his work is of primary importance as the most subtle and exhaustive critique of Foxe's eschatology.

Towards the end of James I's reign Foxe's view of the Christian Prince seemed old-fashioned to two sorts of people: to those who followed the *iure divino* Anglicanism of bishops such as Barlow, Bilson, Bancroft, Carleton and Downame; and to those who followed the centrifugal millenarianism of Thomas Brightman. While the easy-going Low Churchman, Abbott, was archbishop of Canterbury the first group were not influential, the second not systematically persecuted. The accession of Charles I – sceptical, unlike his father, of Foxe's faith in the Godly Prince – marks a decisive change. Laud's supremacy in the Church challenges, not 'Godly Rule', but Foxe's ideal of how to attain it.

1. Mark H. Curtis, 'The Hampton Court Conference and its Aftermath', *History*, XLVI (1961) 1.

2. D. H. Willson, *The Privy Councillors in the House of Commons, 1604–29* (Minneapolis, 1940) *passim*.

3. James I, *Political Works . . .*, ed. C. H. McIlwain (Cambridge, Mass., 1918). This distinction is blurred even in McIlwain's careful introduction.

4. J. N. Figgis, *The Divine Right of Kings*, ed. G. R. Elton (Harper Torchbooks, 1965), especially p. 11, and, for some valuable modifications of Figgis's views by Dr Elton, pp. xxvi–xxxii; *The Stuart Constitution 1603–88*, ed. J. P. Kenyon (Cambridge University Press, 1966) p. 50.

5. N. Cohn, *The Pursuit of the Millennium* (Mercury Books, 1957) pp. 321–78.

6. (Doctor Williams's Library) Baxter MSS. 59.3, f. 115v; 59.5, f. 161v; 59.3, f. 115.

7. 'I was much addicted to the excessive gluttonous eating of apples and pears,' etc., from: Richard Baxter, *Autobiography* (Everyman's Library, 1931) p. 5.

8. John Jewel, *Works* (Cambridge, Parker and Son, 1849) II 916–7; IV 835–7; William Tyndale, *Doctrinal Treatises* (Cambridge, Parker Society, 1848) p. 186; William Tyndale, *Expositions and Notes* (Cambridge, Parker Society, 1849) pp.

270, 280; Edward Grindal, *Remains* (Cambridge, Parker Society, 1843) p. 12; John Bale, *Select Works* (Cambridge, Parker Society, 1849) p. 502; James Pilkington, *Works* (Cambridge, Parker Society, 1848) p. 8.

9. John Foxe, *Acts and Monuments* (London, 1837) VII 466.

10. William Prynne, *Anti-Arminianisme* ... (London, 1629) pp. 85–6.

11. Richard Bancroft, *A Sermon Preached at Paules Cross* (London, 1588).

12. George Carleton, *Jurisdiction, Regall, Episcopal, Papall* (London, 1610) dedicatory epistle, pp. 4, 6, 24, 29, 31, 37, 39, 44.

13. George Downame, *An Extract of a Sermon ... Of the Dignity and Duty of the Ministry* (London, 1608). It is interesting that this sermon should be printed in full in an appendix to George Hickes's tract of 1711, *Two Treatises of the Christian Priesthood*. The eighteenth-century High Churchmen would find their ancestors in the Jacobean divines. Hickes's antipathy to the 'overawed' Tudor bishops, who had allowed the spiritual/temporal distinction to become blurred, was notorious. He went so far as to argue that 'King Henry crucified the Church'.

14. Ibid., pp. lxxxviii, xci, xcv, xcix.

15. Thomas Sparke, *A Brotherly Persuasion to Unitie ...* (London, 1607) p. 78.

16. William Barlow, *An Answere to a Catholike Englishman* (London, 1609) dedicatory epistle, pp. 43, 44, 45, 123.

17. Ibid., dedicatory epistle.

18. George Downame, *Two Sermons ...* (London, 1608) preface.

19. P. Collinson, *The Elizabethan Puritan Movement*; Christopher Hill, *Society and Puritanism in pre-Revolutionary England* (London, Secker and Warburg, 1964).

20. Robert Bolton (1572–1631), a Northamptonshire rector; John Preston (1587–1628), preacher at Lincoln's Inn and Master of Emmanuel College, Cambridge; Richard Sibbes (1577–1635), preacher at Gray's Inn and Master of St Catherine's Hall, Cambridge; John Reynolds (1549–1607), president of Corpus Christi College, Oxford.

21. Richard Baxter, *Five Disputations of Church-Government and Worship* (London, 1659) p. 6.

22. (Doctor Williams's Library) Baxter MSS. 59.1, f. 59; 59.2, f. 2llv.

23. John Humfrey, *A Second Vindication* (London, 1656) dedicatory epistle.

24. Collinson, *The Elizabethan Puritan Movement*, p. 334.

25. George Gillespie, *Aarons Rod Blossoming* ... (London, 1646) p. 585.

26. Alexander Leighton (1568–1649) who suffered mutilation for his radical ecclesiastical writings seven years before the more famous punishment of Prynne, Burton and Bastwick.

27. (Doctor Williams's Library) Baxter MSS. 59.2, ff. 218–19.

28. Bilson's place in the movement is more ambivalent. I have discussed it at length in: 'The Rise and Fall of Bishop Bilson', *The Journal of British Studies*, v 2 pp. 22–32.

29. (Anon.), *An Answere to a Sermon preached ... by George Downame* ... (London, 1609) pp. 5, 36.

30. John Reynolds (?), *Mr Downames Sermon ... Answered and Refuted* ... (London, 1609) pp. 4, 19, 20, 51, 121.

31. Paul Baynes, *The Diocesans Tryall* (London, 1621) p. 66.

32. Sylvester Norris, *The Guide of Faith* (London, 1621) p. 179.

33. Anthony Wood, *Athenae Oxonienses*, ed. Bliss (Oxford, 1817) III 84; Peter Heylyn, *Cyprianus Anglicus* (London, 1668) p. 156.

34. For Puritan hopes, see Thomas Ball, *Life of Preston* (London, 1628); for Laudian fears, see *The Correspondence of John Cosin* ..., ed. G. Ornsby (Surtees Society, LII) 17, 103.

35. William Prynne, *A Breviate of the Prelates Intollerable Usurpations* ... (London, 1637) pp. 122–4.

36. William Bradshaw, *English Puritanisme* (London, 1605) p. 35; *A Protestation of the Kings Supremacie* (London, 1607) p. 16; (Anon.) *The New Man* (London, 1622); Robert Bolton, *Two Sermons* (London, 1635) p. 21.

37. Henry Burton, *Lord Bishops None of the Lords Bishops* (London, 1640) no pagination. My reasons for rejecting the common attribution of this important work to Prynne are set out in 'Prynne, Burton, and the Puritan Triumph,' *Huntington Library Quarterly*, XXVII 2 pp. 103–13.

38. Leonard Busher, *Religious Peace* (London, 1614) in *Tracts on Liberty of Conscience and Persecution 1614–1661*, ed. E. Underhill, pp. 13, 30, 40, 41, 58.

39. Only in one of Prynne's pamphlets, *Romes Masterpiece* (London, 1644) pp. 28–9, does he make a serious intellectual effort to distinguish Laudian from Papist: he calls Laud then 'another Cassander, or middle man betweene an absolute Papist and a reall Protestant'. But until 1641 he consistently distinguished Laudians from moderate Anglicans: even when his ears were being mutilated for a second time in 1637 he went out

of his way to praise Laud's *episcopal* opponent, John Williams: *A New Discovery of the Prelates Tyranny* ... (London, 1641) pp. 43–4.

40. C. H. and K. George, *The Protestant Mind of the English Reformation 1570–1640* (Princeton, University Press, 1961) p. 217.

41. Thomas Brightman, *A Revelation of the Revelation* (3rd edn., Leyden, 1616) pp. 161, 163, 192, 334, 336, 448, 460.

3 Godly Bishop

'Begin with an individual and before you know it you find that you have created a type; begin with a type, and you find that you have created – nothing.'[1] When we discuss Archbishop Laud we begin with a type and usually end with nothing – nothing, that is, except clichés about the abasement of Church before Crown. The type was the creation of Lord Macaulay. Archbishop Laud, 'minuting down his dreams, counting the drops of blood which fall from his nose, watching the direction of the salt, and listening for the note of the screech-owl',[2] becomes, in Macaulay's splendidly contemptuous prose, the type of the royal creature. He becomes a Sir Thomas More upside down: God's good servant, but the king's first. Most modern political historians have been influenced by Macaulay's brilliantly unfair judgement. Thus Godfrey Davies, in his summing-up of Laud in his Oxford History, is Macaulay minus the unfairness, but also minus the brilliance:

> The Anglican leaders were mainly to blame for their own downfall . . . because they sought to buttress the Church by an alliance with the Crown instead of depending on the inherent strength of Anglicanism.[3]

It is undeniably true that Laud did seek to buttress the Church by an alliance with the Crown. So too had Barlow, Bilson, Bancroft and Carleton – the myth-makers of Hampton Court. The real question is whether Laud, unlike them, was prepared to sacrifice the independence of the Church as the price of this alliance. And this is a more open question than either Davies or Macaulay seems to concede.

The first reason why it is an open question is that it was

never put. Charles I was the best Anglican that ever sat upon the English throne. The bishops' worst fears about his father's theology had not been fulfilled. But we have seen that it still remained necessary for Carleton, Downame and their colleagues to remind James about the limits to the powers of a Godly Prince. His son needed no such reminder. He did not see that it was part of *his* function to determine the nature of a 'Godly Rule'. He was willing to leave such matters to Laud. And this not because he was uninterested and a lukewarm Anglican, but because he was passionately interested and a perfervid Anglican. But his was not the Anglicanism of Foxe and Jewel. It was the Anglicanism of Barlow and Bancroft: one which emphasised the primary function of the bishops, ruling by divine right, to define doctrine. In 1637 the Court was buzzing with rumours that, in the course of a private conversation, Charles had flatly denied that he *was* the Head of the Church. Charles put the Jesuits at Court on the defensive on at least two occasions by claiming that they were like the Puritans in failing to recognise that bishops ruled by divine right.[4] Why should his bishops *need* to assert clerical superiority with such a king on the throne? But this did not mean that they had abandoned claims that had been first formulated to meet the crisis provoked by an ailing queen and an alien heir.

Let there by a less accommodating ruler than Charles on the throne and then we would hear a different tune from the Laudian bishops! This was the gist of Stephen Marshall's comment in 1643:

> And I suspect, in case the tables were turned and we had a King endeavouring to take down the bishops... and a Parliament seeking to maintain them, the world would hear another Divinity from many of them who now crie out, that all our defence is damnable.[5]

The weakness of this argument was that less even in 1643 than in the 1630s was it plausible to suppose that the king would endeavour 'to take down the bishops'. It sounded like sour grapes. And yet, by an extraordinary twist of fortune, the tables *were* turned in November 1648. Or, at least, it seemed to the fevered imagination of a couple of Laudian clergymen that they were. Edmund Boughen and Peter Heylyn were both convinced that Charles was about to save monarchy by renouncing bishops. Boughen shrilly pointed out that because bishops ruled by divine right they could not be outed by a royal whim:

> Now if Episcopacy be our Saviours institution, then may no humane power root it up, least they that do it, be rooted out of the land of the living.

Heylyn was equally rude:

> It was the interest of King Charles to maintain Episcopacy, as one of the chief supporters of the Regall Throne ... the King's judgment was corrupted by Partiality, and swayed with interess, which rendered him no fit witness in the present Tryall.[6]

Boughen and Heylyn had misjudged their man. His son was another matter. In 1650 the tables *were* turned: Prince Charles took the Covenant. The resilience with which Anglicans met a crisis that would have shattered a Cranmer, a Gardiner, a Whitgift; later still, the ability of Sheldon to defy the Crown when it attempted an Indulgence to Papists; later still, the bishops' defiance of James II: all are pointers to the danger of reading too much into the sycophancy of the court sermon.

Moreover, it is of interest that Boughen and Heylyn did not concoct something new to meet the exceptional situation in 1648. They only made *explicit* what had been *implicit* in their own writings in the 1630s. Thus, in 1637, Boughen said of the bishops' dependence on the Royal Supremacy: 'But (blessed be God) they hold not only by this, but by an higher tenure.' And, true to this principle, he argued that, in a dispute over obedience, the ultimate court of appeal was archbishop, not king.[7] Heylyn, in the same year, had ducked the question of whether churchmen should continue to obey a king who sought to alter religion:

> his majesties pietie and zeale being too well knowne to give occasions to such queres.

At least until 1648: though, in truth, Heylyn's position was already clear much earlier. Heylyn was sensitive enough to clerical claims to go to even the extraordinary lengths of conceding that the Scottish Presbyterians had a right to object, in 1635, to the Book of Canons being imposed on them without their consent. Heylyn argued that this was 'contrary to the usage of the Church in all Times and Ages'. He showed the limits of princely interference:

> ... as for Canons and Constitutions Ecclesiasticall, if they concerned the whole Church, they were to be advised and framed by Bishops, and other learned men, assembled in a general Council, and testified by the subscription of such Bishops as were then assembled.... And though it could not be denied, but that all Christian Emperors, Kings and Princes reserved a Power into themselves of Ratifying and Confirming all such Constitutions as by the Bishops and Clergy were agreed on, yet still the said Canons and Constitutions were first agreed on by the Bishops and Clergy, before they were tendred to the Sovereign Prince for his ratification.

Moreover, Heylyn explicitly drew on his great Jacobean predecessors. At the show-trial of the Puritan pamphleteers, Prynne, Burton and Bastwick in 1637, Heylyn demonstrated that the bishops' *iure divino* claims were nothing new by direct reference to Bancroft, Bilson and 'many others of those times'. And when Bishop Hall aroused Puritan storms in 1641 by defending episcopacy by divine right Heylyn observed that there was nothing in these controversies that had not already been dealt with by Bilson and Downame.[8]

It is Heylyn's closeness to Laud which makes this evidence so significant. Heylyn was Laud's first biographer, disciple and friend. While it is true that, apart from his attack on the Jesuit, Fisher, Laud wrote very little, what he did write is in striking accord with Heylyn's philosophy. We know that Laud approved of Lancelot Andrewes's *iure divino* claim for episcopacy and that, at his own trial during the Civil War, he conceded that, while the *exercise* of his jurisdiction might be from the king, *the power itself* was 'by Divine apostolical right and unalterable'. If such views were at variance with the teachings of Foxe and Jewel,

Laud warned on another occasion against following their judgements too slavishly:

> ... though these two were very worthy men in their time, yet everything which they say is not by and by the doctrine of the Church of England. And I may upon good reason depart from their judgment in some particulars, and yet not differ from the Church of England.[9]

Joseph Hall was to echo this declaration of independence in 1640:

> ... we cannot prescribe to other men's thoughts; where all is said, men will take liberty (and who can hinder it?) to abound in their own sense.[10]

This similarity was not accidental. When we bemoan Laud's thin contribution to controversy, we sometimes forget Hall's unrepentant defence of episcopacy by divine right in 1640 and 1641.[11] We know now that Laud was at Hall's elbow throughout the writing of his works. They are Laud's vicarious masterpieces. And we find Laud, writing to Hall, pressing his views on the divine sanction of episcopacy and acknowledging his debt to Bilson:

> For Bishop Bilson set out a book in the Queen's time, intitled *The Perpetual Government*. And if the government by bishops be perpetual, as he very learnedly proves through the whole book, it will be hard for any Christian nation to out it.[12]

The idea of a link between Bilson and Laud was to seem preposterous in 1640. In that year, Henry Burton could say to Laud: 'Neither (I suppose) are you of opinion with one a Brother of Winchester.' Why? Because Bilson was then regarded as, *par excellence,* the apologist for godly rebellion.[13] As such, he was at the opposite end of the spectrum from Laud, the royal lackey. To do justice to Bilson's influence on Laud, Burton would have needed to relate Bilson to the other clerical apologists for independence that were discussed in the previous chapter, and then to appreciate that these men were the real begetters of Laudianism.

The 'Laudians' may not have been so tidy and discrete a group as both their champions and detractors tried to make out.[14] But from the correspondence of intimates of Laud like Cosin and Mountague a whiff of something like 'group' solidarity is unmistakably transmitted.[15] It comes over most powerfully in defence of the claims of the Church and is associated, not only with Heylyn, Boughen and Laud but also with other sympathisers like Pocklington, Hoard and Cosin. Pocklington, who developed Carleton's argument about the self-sufficiency of the Church before Constantine, added:

> Miserable were We; if he that now Sitteth Arch-Bishop of Canterbury, could not derive his succession from St. Augustine, St. Augustine from St. Gregory, St. Gregory from St. Peter.

Laud gave explicit approval to Pocklington's thesis; he dismissed the contrary position as 'an upstart Clergy without a calling'.[16] Hoard went further even than Carleton had done in a sermon of 1637: he claimed coactive, *as well as* directive, power for the Church. John Hales had seen the Biblical text, in which Jesus had rebuked his disciples for contending for superiority, as a slap at *iure divino* claims by bishops. Hoard, on the other hand, saw it as 'no arguments for the clipping of the Church wings, more than for the limiting of civill authority'. And he claimed that it was 'the duty of people to submit themselves to the directions and prescriptions of their Bishops and spiritual rulers, who succeed a greater than Moses, Christ and his Apostles'.[17] Most notorious of all was John Cosin who was alleged to have said, in private conversation, that the king had no more power to excommunicate than the man who rubbed Cosin's horse's heels. It is often overlooked that Cosin's denial of this charge is as powerful an assertion of clerical supremacy as any of the other statements that we have quoted![18]

These writers in Laud's circle were rediscovered with some astonishment by eighteenth-century High Churchmen. With some astonishment, for they had assumed that Laud had sold the pass. Behind Macaulay lay White Kennett, assuring the Commons in 1706 that it was in Laud's time that 'Arbitrary Power' in the Monarchy was extolled. And behind White Kennett lay Roger

Mainwaring and Robert Sibthorpe, whose sermons of 1627 gave substance to this charge. But the High Churchman, Thomas Brett, republished in 1714 Edward Boughen's clericalist sermons of 1635 precisely because they showed that there were other Anglicans at that time who did not share the views of Mainwaring and Sibthorpe. Brett bracketed Boughen with Laud, Andrewes and Hall.[19]

Why then did the Mainwarings and Sibthorpes loom so large in the Commons' attacks on the Laudian Church? Not because it was assumed that the *only* effect of Laudianism was the exaltation of the Crown. But that was the effect which seemed to have greatest relevance to the political situation where the enhancement, not the diminution, of the royal prerogative was causing most concern. That concern was reflected in a sermon of Thomas Gataker in 1637. Gataker – in the best traditions of English Nonconformity – acclaimed the divinity of kings, and stressed the importance of the struggles of the Christian Emperor against the Papacy. But he could not leave it there, as his Jacobean predecessors such as Baynes and Reynolds would surely have done. He must also add that kings receive their power from the people, and that subjects ultimately can appeal from kings to God, 'their utmost refuge'.[20] Similarly, in 1641, Henry Parker shared Gataker's alarm at the way in which the *iure divino* claim for episcopacy emasculated the Christian Prince, but was forced, like Gataker, to emphasise that 'Mainwaring's Doctrine is common at Court'. Only in 1645 had he the perspective to see that his fears of Court Divinity had been disproportionate; that the ultimate result of Laudianism was to 'set up and settle an absolute or independent prerogative in the Church to churchmen, which is inconsistent with the prerogative of the Crown'.[21] It was not so easy in the period up to the Civil War to strike this balance. What happened was that fears of clerical supremacy coexisted with fears of royal supremacy, and were never quite submerged by them. And so in the *original charges* against Laud, he was accused on the two counts: of exalting Crown above Parliament and of exalting Church above Crown. But – as Laud was swift to point out – it hardly made for a coherent argument to claim that he was simultaneously engaged in a conspiracy to exalt, and to undermine, the Royal Supremacy.[22] And, in the event, the charge that he was seeking to destroy the Royal Prerogative was quietly dropped. But not the conviction that had originally prompted its inclusion: this continued to exist as a subterranean source of resentment against Laud. We see it surfacing in the reprinting in 1641 of the writings of Jacobean Nonconformists such as Baynes and Reynolds against *iure divino* Anglicanism, in the fears aroused by the appointment of a cleric, Juxon, as Lord Treasurer, and with consistent violence in the pamphleteering of William Prynne.

The Scottish Presbyterians did not attack Laud for his clericalism, but for his sycophancy. Believing in *iure divino* Presbyterianism, they could not share the fears for the civil magistrate expressed by their English counterparts. But this is not the whole explanation; they may have genuinely misunderstood Laud's position. Robert Baillie had certainly drawn attention to the popularity of *iure divino* claims for episcopacy among the Laudians; he noted with alarm the sermon of Pocklington and bracketed him with Hoard and Boughen; he deplored their belief that:

> the dignity of the Episcopall office especially the Bishop of Rome his eminence was as far above the dignity of the Emperours and Kings, as the soule is above the body.

Mountague's writings and Cosin's indiscreet conversation were also noted by Baillie.[23] But Baillie cited John Wemys's work, *De Regis Primatu,* as evidence of the more important tendency in Anglicanism: to exalt the magistrate. Wemys's work supports such an inference: he claimed for the king a power to make canons without the advice of the clergy (a point completely repugnant to Laud and Heylyn)[24]; the king could summon synods of whatever composition he chose; the king could appoint for the government of his Church such spiritual courts and officers as pleased him; the king, not bishops, judged in matters of faith. Wemys's tract was indeed in line with the old imperial tradition of Anglicanism: an inference supported by his frequent citations of Marsilio of Padua.[25] George Gillespie, another Presbyterian Scot, also took Wemys as representative of Laudianism in the exaggerated powers that he conferred on the magistrate. This led him to a fallacious, but significant, conclusion: 'The Tutor which bred up the Erastian error was Arminianism.'[26]

Nothing could be more false. If the group commonly called 'Arminians', who were associated with Laud, have one thing in common, it is not doctrinal rigidity, but anti-Erastianism (in the sense in which Gillespie is using the term). The one distinctive feature of a group that was never closely knit as a coherent party was an intense pride in the Church as an institution. The care that members of the group took to define the independent status of episcopacy was one aspect of a pride which also expressed itself in a determined use of the church courts and in an emphasis on the liturgical and sacramental functions of the church service. One might hold these views and also be critical of the Calvinist doctrine on Predestination; but the one was not a necessary corollary of the other. The great champions of *iure divino* Anglicanism in James's reign, Carleton and Downame, were unbending Calvinists in doctrine. Joseph Hall continued this tradition of High Church Calvinism in the reign of Charles. But there could also be such a thing as Low Church Arminianism. Howson, bishop of Durham, was named by Heylyn as one of the men who laid the foundations for Mountague's doctrinal attack on Calvinism; this did not prevent him from displaying a marked sympathy with the Puritan, Smart, against Cosin on the question of ceremonial innovations.[27]

'Arminianism' is a misleading term in that it implies a coherence in views on church organisation and doctrine that did not exist. Moreover, the doctrinal challenge itself was much more muffled than the term suggests. Andrewes himself had commented on the second of the Lambeth Articles:

> The moving, or efficient, cause of predestination to life is not prevenient faith, or perseverance, or good works, or any other thing that is innate in the predestined person, but only the will of a beneficent God.

Laud's views were similar:

Man lost by sin the integrity of his nature, and can not have light enough to see the way to heaven but by grace.[28]

Mountague rejected Popery because it lacked Scriptural warrant:

> The Originall grounds of Popery are to my understanding, against Reason, have not the warrant from revealed Truth, stand not with the purer practice of prime Antiquity.

These so-called doctrinal innovators may have felt uncomfortable about certain aspects of Predestination – 'fitting rather Schooles than popular cases of auditories' as Mountague put it – but this did not amount to a sustained theological attack on Calvinist dogma.

A recent writer, J. F. H. New, noting the minor part that doctrine plays in the 'Arminian' controversy, suggests that the whole concept of Predestination has been overworked. He comments on the fact that Prynne, ostensibly attacking theological Arminianism, drags in a whole host of complaints against the Laudians that have nothing to do with doctrine. This is true, but it is not for want of trying on Prynne's part. He is very concerned about doctrine – he goes right back to Pelagius to trace the ancestry of Arminianism. But all his ingenuity can tease out only a few contemporary examples of doctrinal deviations – a Barrett here, a Baro there. He is driven to describe parallel deviations that are taking place in the Church under the patronage of Laud: the placing of the Communion table, bowing at the name of Jesus and suchlike innovations.

Now Prynne is typical of other critics of Laud – for instance, of the Commons in their resolution on religion which they drew up on 24 February 1629 – both in the belief that a frontal challenge to Calvinist dogma was taking place, and in a failure to produce adequate documented evidence to support this belief. This does not, as New supposes, mean that Predestination was a minor factor in dividing Anglican from Puritan; this would only be so, if there were a correlation between what divided men from each other and what men *thought* divided them from each other. Doctrinally, the Laudians and their opponents were closer than most Puritans thought. But it was in vain for Mountague to protest that he hadn't read Arminius. As New himself has pointed out, 'the Laudian innovations, in some respects insignificant enough, were symbols of fundamental assumptions that were more clearly felt than articulated'. No assumption was more clearly felt than the one that Laud was pushing the Church of England towards Rome; if it was articulated, however unconvincingly, in the charge of 'Arminianism', this is itself of importance. The paranoid vigilance with which doctrinal Calvinism was defended is proof of the strength, rather than the weakness, of its hold on the popular imagination.

Prynne says, at one point, of Calvinist dogma that 'these were the truths that secured us from the Spanish Armada in '88'. Foxe had seen the present Church of Rome as a 'swerving' from the Apostolic Church; Prynne saw Laudianism as a 'swerving' from true Anglican tradition. First among the errors of the present Church of Rome Foxe had placed her attitude to 'faith and justification'; on the Foxeian thesis of the 'swerving', the deviations in doctrine that Prynne could detect became the more crucial.[29] Arminianism fell into place as proof positive that Laud and his associates were conspiring with Antichrist against the Christian emperor. And perhaps Mountague's greatest crime, in the eyes of his opponents, was not any explicit commitment to Free Will, but his refusal to accept the Foxeian belief that the Papacy *was* Antichrist. He went so far as to accept that the Pope was *one* of many Antichrists; he was not prepared to accept, from the Book of Revelation, that Antichrist could be directly identified with Rome:

> it is in Scripture every where tendred as a Prophecy; and therefore a Mystery sealed up, obscure, not manifested, not to bee understood, but by evident and plaine event, without divine revelation.[30]

Item 26 in the Articles against Cosin shows how inflammatory such views were:

> But you, John Cosin, lyke a saucy fellow, changed Dr Whyte's words, or the words of Mr Montague approved by him, from it, that 'The Turke is Antichrist *as well as* the Pope'

to 'The Turke is Antichrist *rather than* the Pope'. And this
you did schismatically and seditiously, to shew your love to
the Pope, and to vent your phanaticall opinion that the Pope
is not the great Antichrist of whom St. Paule speaketh, and St.
John also in the Revelation.[31]

Opponents rightly sensed that Laud and his associates were
moving away from Foxe's centripetal millenarianism. The
Christian Emperor was being dethroned – with Charles I's smil-
ing approval. But there was no vacuum left. Laud may have been
sceptical of Foxe's 'Godly Ruler', but not of Foxe's 'Godly Rule'.
As one commentator has pointed out, 'Laud's emphasis on the
uniqueness and worthiness of the English Church was a nation-
alist counterblast to the Puritans, who had always stressed
England's mission as the chosen race, the leader of European
Protestantism: in place of the Elect Nation Laud offered the
Elect Church'.[32]

The negative side of Laudianism – the repudiation of Foxe,
the Elect Nation, the martyr-bishops, the Emperor Constantine
– aroused the wrath of contemporary opponents, but should not
blind us to the fact that Laudianism did have a positive side:
the Laudians dethroned the Elect Nation only to enthrone the
Elect Church. When a Laudian bishop entered a Puritan minister's house and saw pictures of Marian martyrs on the wall, he
commented: 'What doest thou with the picture of these fanati-
call and brainesicke fellowes in thy chamber?' The story comes
from a bigoted Puritan source.[33] We may doubt the literal
accuracy of the story; not the genuineness of the anxiety that
prompted its telling. It was notable that, at Laud's funeral sermon, he lovingly recalled his saintly predecessors at Canterbury
– but omitted to mention Cranmer.[34] Yet it did not follow that,
because Laud and his associates disliked Foxe and the martyrs,
they were untouched by millenarian hopes. It was a Laudian
who argued that the Beast would only be overcome by a 'splen-
did visibility' greater than Rome itself: episcopacy by divine
right.[35] It is unusual to find Laud or his followers making such
a direct reference to the Book of Revelation, although it should
be remembered that Mountague had been sceptical of the view

that the Papacy was *the* Antichrist, not that it was *an* Antichrist; Cosin, likewise, 'lyke a saucy fellow' had cast the Turk rather than the Pope in that role, but had not found the role itself incredible. And if the Laudians rejected a godly discipline under Constantine, they welcomed the idea itself of a godly discipline. Their refusal to rest content with the *iure humano* justification for episcopacy is only fully intelligible against the background of millenarian hopes that they shared with their critics.

It is understandable that their critics should be slow to give them credit for this aspiration. An exception is Edward Johnson, who saw that Puritans and Laudians were united in the *ends* that they followed. From this, he drew the sensible conclusion that more attention must be paid to the *means*:

> ... all men that expect the day (of Judgment) must attend the means: for such hath been and is the absurdity of many, that they make semblance of a very zealous affection to see the glorious work of our Lord Christ herein, and yet themselves uphold, or at best side with those that uphold some part of Antichrists Kingdome: and therefore the Lordly Prelacy may pray for his fall till their lungs are spent, and their throats grow dry.[36]

Naturally, an opponent would dismiss such millenarian longings in the Laudians as counterfeit; what is rare is to find such longings recognised at all. Such longings find scant recognition in those historians who have been content to describe Laudianism simply in terms of abasement before the Crown. On the other hand, those historians who have concerned themselves with the *social*, rather than the *political*, implications of Laudianism, have emphasised the very positive role that Laud envisaged for his Church. And, in that sphere, they have noted a curious affinity of purpose between Laud and his enemies. As Professor Trevor-Roper has remarked:

> Did English Puritans denounce the unloveliness of lovelocks, gay clothes, the drinking of toasts? The Archbishop forbade long hair in Oxford, reformed clerical abuses, urged war on alehouses.[37]

Another historian has pointed to the strange parallel between the vices singled out for attention by the Dedham *classis* in the 1580s, the Westminster Assembly in the 1640s and – neatly between these peaks of English puritan discipline – Laud's visitation articles to the diocese of St David's.[38] Even Macaulay, the most eloquent advocate of the view of Laud as a royal lapdog, could not ignore passages in Laud's correspondence with Strafford that conveyed piety and a sense of duty to God:

> He regrets to hear that a church is used as a stable and that the benefices of Ireland are very poor. He is desirous that, however small a congregation may be, service should be regularly performed.

Macaulay entertained for Laud 'a more unmitigated contempt than for any other character in our history'. He thought that Parliament was too merciful in merely executing such a man; he would have sent him to Oxford. He had no doubts, then, that this supposed piety merely cloaked self-interest:

> All this may be very proper; and it may be very proper that an alderman should stand up for the tolls of his borough, and an East India director for the charter of his Company. But it is ridiculous to say that these things indicate piety and benevolence.

Was it so ridiculous? The lie to Macaulay's sneer comes direct from Laud's diary. Macaulay could never look at it 'without forgetting the vices of his heart in the imbecility of his intellect'.[39] The diary, however, repays close attention as an extraordinary, moving record of one man's hopes and fears. It is an authentic puritan document. And Puritan opponents, who loathed Laud's innovations in church ceremonies, were curiously blind to the bonds that united him with them. This led them into a serious blunder in 1645. They seized his diary and published it in the hope of discrediting him. Instead, Laud's Puritan opponents found themselves strangely drawn to a man, possessed like them of a vision, assured of its rectitude, but driven to record with painful honesty the temptations and backslidings on the path to that goal. Almost against their will, William Walwyn and Henry Robinson were impressed by the 'signes of a morall noble pious

minde' in his diary, although they added an important rider:
'according to such weak principles as hee had been bred up
in'.[40] In other words: they abhorred what he *stood* for, not what
he *strove* for. Conversely we shall see that after 1660 Laud's
followers might restore what he stood for, but they could not
restore what he strove for. Episcopacy was restored, but not the
ideal of the Unity of Jerusalem nor the instruments – the Court of
Star Chamber, the Court of High Commission, the clerical visitations – to implement that ideal. The Restoration Church was not,
except in superficial matters, Laudian.

The power that Laud sought for his Church was to be used
to bring closer to realisation the ideal of a 'Godly Rule'. This is
where the similarity of ends between Laudians and their opponents is of such importance. Mountague told Cosin, in a letter
on 17 January 1625, that an opponent had told him that 'I was
no Puritan in my writings but in my actions'.[41] This was because
Mountague had quit the Deanery of Hereford on conscientious
grounds. But it also points to a wider truth about Laud's clericalism; the ends that he was seeking to implement – the raising of
ethical standards among clergy and laity, the abolition of pluralism and absenteeism and the like – were those sought with equal
fervour by his Puritan opponents. Laud sought to combat the
situation described by Richard Baxter in his autobiography:

> In the village where I was born there was four readers suc-
> cessively in six years time, ignorant men, and two of them
> immoral in their lives, who were all my schoolmasters. In the
> village where my father lived there was a reader of about
> eighty years of age that never preached, and had two churches
> about twenty miles distant. His eyesight failing him, he said
> Common Prayer without book; but for the reading of the
> psalms and chapters he got a common thresher and day-
> labourer one year, and a tailor another year (for the clerk
> could not read well); and at last he had a kinsman of his own
> (the excellentest stage-player in all the country, and a good
> gamester and good fellow) that got Orders and supplied
> one of his places. After him another younger kinsman, that
> could write and read, got Orders. And at the same time another
> neighbour's son that had been a while at school turned minis-
> ter, one who would needs go further than the rest, and ven-

tured to preach (and after got a living in Staffordshire) and
when he had been a preacher about twelve or sixteen years
he was fain to give over, it being discovered that his Orders
were forged by the first ingenious stage-player. After him
another neighbour's son took Orders, when he had been a
while an attorney's clerk, and a common drunkard, and tippled
himself into so great poverty that he had no other way to live.
It was feared that he and more of them came by their Orders
the same way with the forementioned person. These were the
schoolmasters of my youth (except two of them) who read Common Prayer on Sundays and Holy-Days, and taught school
and tippled on the weekdays, and whipped the boys, when
they were drunk, so that we changed them very oft. Within a
few miles about us were near a dozen more ministers that were
near eighty years old apiece, and never preached; poor ignorant
readers, and most of them of scandalous lives. Only three or
four constant competent preachers lived near us, and those
(though conformable all save one) were the common marks of
the people's obloquy and reproach, and any that had but gone
to hear them, when he had no preaching at home, was made
the derision of the vulgar rabble under the odious name of a
Puritan.[42]

The thirst for a 'Godly Rule' is intelligible against such a
background; Baxter's account is a terrible indictment of Archbishop Abbott.

And yet it was Laud, not Abbott, who aroused the censure of
Puritans. Why? Abbott's indolence had a curious double effect:
its laxity stimulated the growth of a Puritan criticism, but its
laxity also allowed this criticism to exist within the broad framework of a permissive Church. Under Abbott, the unity of
Jerusalem existed, but it was more unity than it was Jerusalem.
It is notable in Baxter's account that, of the three or four 'constant competent preachers', only one found conformity to the
Church intolerable. William Ames spoke of the 'thousands in
England' whose views were close to the Separatists but who remained 'members of the ordinary parishes there'. Dr Collinson
has suggested that the phenomenon of non-separating congregationalism – with its 'prophesyings', 'exercises' and 'repetitions'
rooted in the family and household – was a vital element in
Elizabethan Anglicanism, and was in embryonic form the 'con-

gregational way' of the seventeenth century. The congregationalism of the 1640s in part sprang from the earlier group withdrawals
into smaller gatherings, *within the parish structure*.[43] What was
this but 'the setting and going apart' counselled by Brightman in
order 'to preserve any thing intire sincere and sound'?[44] Within a
framework as indulgent as Abbott's, it was possible for this
implicit congregationalism not to become *explicit*. Dr Collinson
describes a rather touching scene :

> At Aythorp Roding, on a typical occasion, the godly met
> in the house of one Davies, 'to the number of ten persons or
> thereabouts of his kindred and neighbours, being invited
> thither to supper'. Over the meal, 'they then conferred to-
> gether of such profitable lessons as they had learned that day
> at a public catechizing'. After supper, some 'attended to one
> that read in the Book of Martyrs'. . . .[45]

There was a tension between theory and practice; between the
'church-type' theory of the Book of Martyrs – with its martyr-
bishops and Godly Prince – and the 'sect-type' practice of the
congregation at Aythorp Roding.[46] This tension was concealed
by the latitudinarianism of Abbott. As Baxter himself acknowledged :

> Discipline I wanted in the Church, and saw the sad effects
> of its neglect; but I did not then understand that the very
> frame of diocesan prelacy excluded it, but thought it had been
> only the bishops' personal neglects.[47]

Leonard Busher – the Baptist in James I's reign, pleading for
toleration – began with the premise that there were already many
religions in the country; any effort to dragoon them into one
tidy unit would destroy the unity that it was intended to promote :

> Because if there be many religions in the land, as it is well
> known there are, then it will come to pass, through the con-
> tinuance of persecution, that many religions will be continued
> in the church; seeing all are forced to church, who bring their
> religions with them as well as their bodies.[48]

What Busher was asking for was a continuation of the system

whereby men paid lip-service to the idea of one Church of England, while in practice they went their separate ways about achieving a 'Godly Rule'.

This Laud could not do. The unity of Jerusalem – as he made clear in his sermon on the opening of Parliament of 6 February 1626 – implied two things. Unity in itself was desirable, not merely as an *end* in itself but as a *means* to a greater end: the building of Jerusalem. Unity was the prerequisite of the Heavenly City, but in pursuing the means Laud did not lose sight of the end:

> For thither the tribes go up, even the tribes of the Lord, to the testimony of Israel, to give thanks unto the name of the Lord. For there are the seats of judgement; even the thrones of the Home of David.[49]

We find a Mr Claphamson of York writing to Cosin on 16 October 1625: 'I make no doubte but your Worship shall fynd men in this Circuite diversely mynded, and of severall constitucions.'[50] It was precisely this diversity which was tolerable to men like Laud and Cosin, with their vision of what a united Church should be doing.

Macaulay was wrong then to see Laud's oppressive acts as 'the luxuries in which a mean and irritable disposition indulges itself from day to day, the excesses natural to a little mind in a great place'.[51] On the contrary: they derived from that vision of a 'Godly Rule' which he shared with his victims.

1. F. Scott Fitzgerald, *The Diamond as Big as the Ritz and Other Stories* (Penguin, 1964) p. 139.

2. Lord Macaulay, *Critical and Historical Essays* (London, Routledge, 1897) I 168.

3. Godfrey Davies, *The Early Stuarts, 1603–1660,* vol. ix in 'Oxford History of England' (Oxford, Clarendon Press, 1937; 2nd edn. 1959) pp. 77–8.

4. G. Albion, *Charles I and the Court of Rome* (London, Burns, Oates and Washbourne, 1935) pp. 402, 405, 407. As Albion points out, Charles had a genuine controversial point against

the Catholics. The Council of Trent had been noncommittal on the question of whether bishops held a *iure divino* warrant. The discussion provoked heated debate, and so the sixth Canon avoided reference to their source of jurisdiction. Alexander Leighton, *An Appeale to the Parliament* (London, 1628) p. 28, was one Puritan critic who gleefully drew attention to Romish confusion on this issue.

5. Stephen Marshall, *A Copy of a Letter ...* (London, 1643) p. 12.

6. Edward Boughen, *Mr Gerees Case of Conscience Sifted* (London, 1648) p. 20; Peter Heylyn, *Extraneus Valpulans* (London, 1656) p. 168.

7. Edward Boughen, *A Sermon Concerning Decencie and Order in the Church* (London, 1638) pp. 17, 22, 23.

8. Peter Heylyn, *A Briefe and Moderate Answer* (London, 1637) pp. 37, 64; *Cyprianus Anglicus*, p. 301; *The Historie of Episcopacie* (London, 1642) preface.

9. William Laud, *Works*, III 199, 200; IV 310–11, 226; *Calendar State Papers Domestic, Charles I*, CCCXXXII 87–8.

10. Joseph Hall, *An Humble Remonstrance ...* (London, 1640) p. 26. Downame in this, as in so many other matters, had given the lead to both Laud and Hall. He pointed out that, if bishops were now better informed than their Tudor predecessors had been about the nature of their function, 'would it follow that their late thoughts which commonly are the wiser were false and worthie to be confuted?': George Downame, *A Defence of the Sermon*, I 6.

11. Joseph Hall, *An Humble Remonstrance ...*; *Episcopacy by Divine Right ...* (London, 1640); *A Letter Lately Sent by a Reverend Bishop ...* (London, 1642).

12. Laud, *Works ...*, IV 310–11.

13. Henry Burton, *A Replie to a Relation of that Conference ...* (London, 1640) p. 296. The process by which Thomas Bilson – the apologist for *iure divino* episcopacy – became the Roundhead darling is discussed in my 'The Rise and Fall of Bishop Bilson', pp. 22–32.

14. Sir John Lamb: Laud, 4 October 1641: 'You would be ruled by nobody, nor communicate yourself to any that I know, nor make yourself any part at Court, but stood upon yourself: it may be that was your fault rather.' (*Calendar State Papers Domestic, Charles I, 1640–1641*, p. 131.)

15. *The Correspondence of John Cosin, passim.*

16. John Pocklington, *Altare Christianum* (London, 1637) pp. 33, 34; Laud, *Works ...*, IV 340.

17. Samuel Hoard, *The Churches Authority Asserted* (London, 1637) pp. 41, 44, 45, 62; John Hales, *A Tract Concerning Schisme* (London, 1642) p. 13.

18. *The Correspondence of John Cosin*, pp. 147–50.

19. We saw, in the previous chapter, how Downame had been rediscovered by Hickes in 1711; three years later, Brett rediscovered Boughen. Both Brett and Hickes may have been anxious to challenge White Kennett's sermon of 1706: 'It must be confess'd that the Principles of Arbitrary Power and a single Will and Pleasure above the Laws of the Land, were never Preach'd up till at the beginning of those unhappy Times when the Preachers were firstly censured by the Parliament.' But which preachers? White Kennett gives a marginal reference – inevitably – to: Roger Mainwaring, *Religion and Alegiance* (London, 1627); Robert Sibthorpe, *Apostolike Obedience* (London, 1627). One sometimes has a nightmarish feeling that they were the only two preachers giving sermons in Laudian England!

20. Thomas Gataker, *Gods Parley With Princes* ... (London, 1637) pp. 86, 88, 99, 101.

21. Henry Parker, *A Discourse Concerning Puritans* ... (London, 1641), pp. 50–2, and *Ius Regum* ... (London, 1645) p. 27.

22. Laud, *Works* ..., IV 156. Thanks to the availability now of the papers of John Browne, Clerk of the Parliament, in the House of Lords Record Office (Braye MSS, *Proceedings Against Strafford and Laud*) it is possible to reconstruct the trial of Laud. I suggest in my *Marginal Prynne* (London, Routledge, 1963) pp. 119–37, that the motive behind Prynne's alterations in *his* record of the trial is an attempt to present it as an indictment of Laud's exaltation of the Church rather than of his exaltation of the Crown.

23. Robert Baillie, *The Life of William now Lord Arch-Bishop of Canterbury Examined* (London, 1643): this is the third edition of his *The Canterburians Self-Conviction* (London, 1640), with a new title: pp. 38–9, 40, 50, 115, 124–5, 130–1.

24. Peter Heylyn, *The Historie of Episcopacie* ..., II 81; Laud, *Works* ..., IV 352.

25. John Wemys, *De Regis Primatu* ... (Edinburgh, 1623) pp. 64, 119. Cf. F. A. Yates, '*Queen Elizabeth as Astraea*', pp. 43–4, for Marsilio's services to imperial propaganda.

26. George Gillespie, *Aarons Rod Blossoming* ... p. 163. In 1646 the Presbyterian, Thomas Edwards, pointed out that Arminians' exaltation of the magistrate in the United Provinces meant little, as was shown by their changed attitude after the findings of the Synod of Dort: Thomas Edwards, *Gangraena*

(London, 1646) pp. 47–9. The assumption is there still that Arminianism and Erastianism are related, even although the sincerity of the Arminian is impugned.

27. Peter Heylyn, *Cyprianus Anglicus* ... p. 126; *The Correspondence of John Cosin*, pp. 203–4, 206. Arminius himself was closer in doctrine to Calvin than, say, a humanist colleague like Coornhert was: see C. Bangs, 'Arminius and the Reformation', *Church History*, 30 (1961) pp. 155–70.

28. Quoted by J. F. H. New, *Anglican and Puritan* (London, A. & C. Black, 1964) pp. 12, 111. New argues usefully that the boundaries between Anglican and Puritan on Predestination are arbitrary. He seems to strain his case by going on (p. 15) to argue that Predestination was only 'a minor doctrine': almost as if the term 'Arminian' had been coined by later historians such as Professor Haller rather than by seventeenth-century contemporaries!

29. William Prynne, *Anti-Arminianisme* ..., p. 139; Foxe, *Acts and Monuments* I 9, 72.

30. Richard Mountague, *Appello Caesarem* (London, 1625) p. 146.

31. *The Correspondence of John Cosin*, p. 196.

32. J. P. Kenyon, *The Stuart Constitution* (Cambridge University Press, 1966) p. 147.

33. John Bastwick, *Letany* (London, 1637) p. 15.

34. Noted by C. V. Wedgwood, *The King's War, 1641–1647* (London, Collins, 1958) p. 401.

35. (Doctor Williams's Library) Baxter MSS. 59.3, f. 113– f. 114.

36. *The Puritans*, eds. P. Miller and T. Johnson (Harper Torchbooks, 1965) I 160.

37. H. R. Trevor-Roper, 'General Crisis of the Seventeenth Century' in *Crisis in Europe 1560–1660*, ed. T. Aston (London, Routledge, 1965) p. 80.

38. J. F. H. New, *Anglican and Puritan*, p. 22.

39. Lord Macaulay, *Critical and Historical Essays*, I 167, 168.

40. William Walwyn, *A Helpe to the Right Understanding of a Discourse Concerning Independency* ... (London, 1645) p. 2; Henry Robinson, *The Falsehood of Mr William Pryn's Truth Triumphing* ... (London, 1645) p. 9.

41. *The Correspondence of John Cosin*, p. 46.

42. Richard Baxter, *Autobiography*, pp. 3–4.

43. P. Collinson, 'The Godly: Aspects of Popular Protestantism in Elizabethan England' in *Papers Presented to the Past and Present Conference on Popular Religion* (1966) pp. 11, 18.

Collinson suggests that decisions to emigrate, as well as to separate, may have originated from group, rather than individual,
decisions. 'Prophesyings' were the gathering of preaching clergy
for public conference; 'exercises' restricted public business at
such meetings to a single sermon; 'repetitions' were a form of
catechising in households in which the doctrine delivered in earlier
sermons could be rehearsed: see Collinson, p. 10.

44. Brightman, *The Revelation of St John*, p. 448.

45. Collinson, 'The Godly: . . .', pp. 13–14.

46. The 'church-type' ideal glorifies the institutional character
of the Church, and the need – on a Calvinist view – to *discipline*
the reprobate majority. The 'sect-type' ideal glorifies the gathering
into separate communities of the pure and the need to *withdraw*
from the company of the reprobate. See: Ernest Troeltsch, *The
Social Teaching of the Christian Churches* (London, Allen &
Unwin, 1931) pp. 622–3; A. S. P. Woodhouse, *Puritanism and
Liberty*, p. 36.

47. Baxter, *Autobiography*, p. 17.

48. Leonard Busher, *Religion's Peace* (London, 1614) in *Tracts
on Liberty of Conscience and Persecution 1614–1661*, ed. E.
Underhill (London, Hanserd Knollys Society, 1846) p. 30.

49. Kenyon, *The Stuart Constitution*, p. 153.

50. *The Correspondence of John Cosin*, p. 81.

51. Lord Macaulay, *Critical and Historical Essays*, I 168.

4 Godly People

For Anglicans the crucial happening in 1641 was the destruction of Laudianism. Away went censorship, away went Star Chamber and the Court of High Commission, away went imposition of oaths, away went searching visitations, away went the claim that bishops ruled by divine right – and away went the archbishop himself to a prison cell. Laudianism had perished; with indecent haste, Anglicans set about the task of burial. A solitary mourner was Joseph Hall: his writings, which were intended to be the classic apologia for Laudianism, became its epitaph.' Later Laud's biographer, Peter Heylyn, was to claim that the silence of Hall's colleagues was prompted by a desire 'not to robbe him of the glory of a sole encounter'.² This was pure fantasy: the characteristic feature of Anglican writing in 1641 is not chivalry but defensiveness. In the debate on the Root and Branch Bill in the Commons, Benjamin Rudyerd set the tone for the Anglican response when he disowned bad bishops such as Laud and his associates and at the same time pointed out that 'we have some good bishops still, who doe preach every Lords Day'.³ With pride, Rudyerd and other non-Laudians pointed to the contribution of the martyr-bishops in the past. Anglicans belatedly rediscovered Foxe. Puritans were unimpressed: witness the stinging attacks on the martyrs – and by implication on Foxe – in the writings of Milton, Prynne, Smectymnuus, Thomas and Fiennes in 1641.⁴

Yet we have seen that these were the very men who sang the martyrs' praises loudest in the years before the Civil War. Was this cant? No: we must realise that the moderate Anglicans were only superficially offering a restatement of Foxe in 1641.

Anglicans were rediscovering the attractions of the Elizabethan Church, the martyr-bishops and the civil ruler, *but divorced from the millenarian context of Foxe's history*. Cranmer, Latimer and Ridley were extolled as good men who were also bishops – a mere coincidence, sneered Fiennes – but their part in bringing about the downfall of Antichrist was not equally underlined. Moderate Anglicans praised decent, orderly government, a preaching clergy, respect for the magistrate. Should not this have been enough for the Nonconformist reared on Foxe? Now it is true that, at the Restoration, Nonconformists would look back on this time with nostalgia. In the crucial debate of the Restoration Church settlement on the King's Declaration of 1660, they would emphasise the concessions that 'good' bishops such as Williams and Usher had been prepared to make in 1641.[5] And they would be answered with pitiless accuracy by Anglicans such as Roger L'Estrange: these were the very bishops who were scorned by the Nonconformists of 1641.[6] The truth was that, by 1661, the Nonconformists had lowered their aspirations; like the Anglicans after Laud – but twenty years later than them – they had given up apocalyptic visions.

But not in 1641. The Anglican case, whatever its incidental virtues, had one basic flaw: it was dull. To understand why this defect should be so disabling one must examine more closely the mentality of the ministers who roared so loudly for 'root and branch'. And, if we are honest, we must own up to ignorance on certain important points. Dr Pearl has shown how vital was the role of London 'root and branch' ministers in securing the City for Puritanism in 1641.[7] Similarly, Professor Hexter has shown their value in linking mob demonstrations with Pym's control of Parliamentary strategy.[8] Yet we are more familiar with their services *as a group* than we are with the philosophy that sustained them *as individuals*. We still lack good individual studies of ministers who were as important as Burges, Marshall, Calamy, Case, Newcomen and Palmer undoubtedly were. It is therefore possible to draw widely different inferences from their sermons in 1641.

On one view, they are simply harbingers of Presbyterianism.

Their pressure for a Covenant, for an Assembly of Divines, for a 'root and branch' rejection of episcopacy, their friendly links with Scottish ministers: all tie up neatly with the thesis of collusion with Scottish Presbyterianism. It is true that this does not marry well with the respect for the civil magistrate that, we have seen, characterised English Nonconformity in the earlier period. But it could be argued that this respect itself was merely a mask imposed by persecution: this would be true of a pamphleteer like John Bastwick. Where the argument seems weakest is when we look forward, rather than back: to the notable lack of enthusiasm among English ministers for a Covenant and Assembly of Divines that would simply reflect Scottish desires; to their reluctance, once the Assembly had been set up at Westminster, to commit themselves to a Presbyterian solution; to the bitter comments that their conduct provoked from Presbyterian Scots such as Robert Baillie.

These points make plausible an alternative hypothesis: that English Puritanism never severed its historic links with the civil magistrate. On this view, the Covenant and the Westminster Assembly were nothing more than a Scottish rape. The historian, W. A. Shaw, for instance, saw them as the price that the English had to pay for Scottish military help; when the need for that help receded, the theocratic claims of the Westminster Assembly of Divines could be formally rejected.[9]

What support is given to this argument by the sermons of 'root and branch' ministers in 1641? First, there is certainly no commitment to Presbyterianism. Second, there are many deferential remarks in their sermons to Parliament. William Bridge called Parliament 'a quiver, full of chosen and polished shafts for the Lord's work' and Cornelius Burges spoke of 'the most accomplished, best united and most successful and glorious House of Commons that ever sate in that High Court'. Phrases like these prompted one historian, Mrs E. W. Kirby, to conclude that 'throughout all the sermons the dependence of the forces of righteousness upon Parliament was stressed' and that 'the tone of the sermons was, then, Erastian'.[10]

Several criticisms of this thesis may be made. First, it is to place too much emphasis on the *manner* of the sermons. This was one of Baillie's criticisms of the English style of preaching:

> The way here of all preachers, even the best, has been to speak before the parliament with so profound a reverence as truly took all edge from their exhortations.[11]

Baillie exempted Palmer and Hill from these criticisms; they preached 'Scottish and free sermons'. But there is no substantial difference *in content* between Palmer and Hill and the other ministers; only *in presentation*. One minister owned up, with a refreshing candour, to the need to utter 'soft and silken phrases' in praise of the magistrate:[12] these phrases should not be taken at more than their face value. Otherwise one could do as one contemporary, Thomas Coleman, did: make a careful collection of all the extravagant praises of the civil magistrate in the sermons of ministers such as Hill, Palmer, Wilson, Burges, Marshall and Spurstow. Coleman's collection culminates in a eulogy on monarchy from Thomas Case. Coleman noted that this was Erastianism, 'a step higher than ever I or Erastus himself went'. Coleman rightly saw, in the identification of Case as an Erastian, the *reductio ad absurdum* of such reasoning.[13] For Case was implacably theocratic. One writer, in the Civil War, told how Case led a group of ministers into the Commons in 1643 'and desired to be heard, and so delivered some reasons they had, in the behalf of the City, against a Cessation of arms and a Treaty'.[14] This was the man who asked why the truth and power derived from Christ *should* wait at Parliament doors.[15] When, in June 1641, Sir Edward Dering turned against the Root and Branch Bill that he had himself introduced a month before, he complained of the ministers' response:

> Art thou for us or our adversaries? So said one of the usual blacke walkers in Westminster Hall. Another of our Parliament-Pressing Ministers after I had delivered my sense upon Episcopacy in the House came to me and told me plainely, That my conscience was not so good as in the beginning of the Parliament.[16]

In a marginal note, Dering describes the clerical gadfly as 'T.C.':

almost certainly Case. And as Coleman shrewdly remarked on
Case and other 'Parliament-Pressing Ministers':

> . . . it is well known these are not Erastians in their opinions. I
> grant it. But what are they in their words?

But Mrs Kirby is wrong even to think that the ministers *were*
consistently discreet. Marshall warned on one occasion that, if
the Long Parliament withdrew itself from God's work, 'deliverance shall come to Gods people another way'; Case said that 'God
can do his work without a Parliament'; Goodwin told Members
of Parliament that 'if you will not doe it, God will doe it without you.... Reformation will arise some other way'; Harris
warned that 'we have too long Idolized Parliaments'; Calamy
stressed that Parliament was 'not the Authors and Fountaines'
but only 'the Messengers of the good things we enjoy'; Marshall
boasted to the Commons: 'I speak in the name of a great God,
before whom you are but so many grasshoppers, his potheards,
his poore sinfull creatures.'[17] If this is 'the dependence of the
forces of righteousness upon Parliament', it takes a curious form.

But even if the ministers were more independent of Parliament
than Mrs Kirby had supposed, she still has a trump card: at least
they do not commit themselves to a Presbyterian alternative, and
in that sense have not severed themselves from their traditional
willingness to work for reform within the Church of England.
This was the view that Richard Baxter put most forcibly in a
letter to Edward Eccleston in 1673:

> And I suppose you, though young, not ignorant how Hookers
> principles began our warres . . ., that was a parliament of Epis-
> copall men and Erastians, and an Army of such Comanders
> that began it, and the Westminster Assembly were almost all
> conformists.[18]

And, consistent with this view, Baxter sought from Burges –
and obtained – an assurance that he never had in mind the total
destruction of episcopacy; this was in 1659.[19] Now it was understandable that Baxter and Burges should, at a later date, be
anxious to play down the extent of their earlier radicalism. And in
one respect Burges had a clear conscience: he had not been a

slavish follower of the Scots; he had been critical of details in the Solemn League and Covenant.[20] If the criterion of a radical is a willingness to ape the Scots, Burges was no radical. But, in all other respects, Burges and his fellow-ministers *were* radical: what is striking about Burges's opening sermon to the Long Parliament is not, as Professor Haller seems to suppose, that it was preached on Elizabeth's accession day,[21] but that he should refuse to invest the Elizabethan Church with significance and should stress instead the incomplete nature of the Reformation.[22] What emerges in 1641 is a clear division between those who argue for the retention of an episcopacy, shorn of Laud and the claim of bishops to rule by divine right, respecting the civil magistrate, the Elizabethan Church and the martyr-bishops and, on the other hand, those who press – like Burges – for a 'root and branch' destruction of episcopacy, a total reformation and the need for zeal.[23]

In November 1641 Sir Edward Dering had warned the Commons about the dangers of a 'godly' solution. By this time Dering was arguing for a moderate episcopacy against Burges and his colleagues. But it is interesting that Dering does not pretend that his opponents *are* Presbyterians or Independents. He knows that in the England of 1641 there are some Presbyterians and Independents, very few of whom are sitting in the Commons:

> Mr. Speaker, There is a certaine, new-born un-seen, ignorant, dangerous, desperate way of Independency; Are we, Sir, for the independent way? Nay (Sir) are we for the elder brother of it, the Presbyteriall form? I have not yet heard any one Gentleman within these walls stand up and assert his thoughts here for either of these ways.

Yet Dering had the wit to see that the absence of a straightforward advocacy of Presbyterianism or Independency did nothing to diminish the prospects of the ultimate triumph of one or other of these movements:

> and yet (Sir) we are made the Patrons and Protectors of those so different, so repugnant, Innovations.[24]

How could patronage take place without commitment? Dering had an explanation to offer. It is an extremely plausible one. It has the additional advantage of giving a consistency to Dering's own actions in 1640 and 1641; but that is by itself no reason for ruling it out of court. Dering's argument, which he brought out in January 1642, runs along these lines: between November 1640 and May 1641 it was possible to press zealously for total reformation without being a radical; after May 1641 this was no longer true, since the protest movement had by then been taken over by an activist leadership. This then was the apology of a fellow-traveller.[25] Unwittingly he and other English Protestants had played into the hands of the committed. What was the significance of May 1641? That was the date in which the Root and Branch Bill had been introduced. Until then, Dering and men like him could, in their frenzy against Laud, appear to be anti-Anglican when they were only anti-Laudian. It is important to realise why Dering should be so anxious to make his case. He had been the man who actually introduced the Root and Branch Bill, along with an elegant quotation from Ovid. Clarendon, who had not much time for Dering, believed that the chance to display classical learning was perhaps his greatest motive in introducing the Bill.[26] Yet Dering's argument closely attunes with Clarendon's own view of the English Puritans of 1640 and 1641: they knew what they didn't want (Laud), without knowing what they did want.[27] Their violent language obscured the fuzziness of their ideas; they acted as the Trojan Horse for the Presbyterian Scots.

Dering could thus argue in 1642 that he was the constant champion of zeal. It was his opponents, not he, who had changed: 'Whilst they are floating, I stand steady, wondering to what coast they are bound.'[28] May 1641 was the traumatic break for Dering; the Root and Branch Bill exposed, for the first time, that his radical colleagues were now embarking on a different voyage. The 'Parliament-pressing' ministers could reproach him with a bad conscience when he proposed his 'primitive episcopacy' a month after the Root and Branch Bill; his conscience was clear. He had always believed in a moderate episcopacy. Peter Heylyn had indeed seen Dering as representative of the gentry class in Kent, who had been sympathetic to Archbishop Abbott but who had been alienated by Laud.[29] Dering was saying that this was quite simply his position in the early months of 1641. The main reason that 'some thought me as fain for ruine as themselves' was that 'I struck at the tallest Cedar on the Churches Lebanon'. In other words, the zeal with which he proceeded against Laud was a false index to his opinions. His bitterness had a localised application: 'I did not dreame at that time of extirpation and abolition of any more than his Archiepiscopacy.'[30] Nor were the 'rooters' themselves clearer in their aims initially. It was by a policy of drift that English Puritanism came to 'root and branch'.

'Drift' is not the term that we would use of the London ministers' activities at this time, as they appear to us through the researches of Dr Pearl. It is just possible, even if unlikely, that highly sophisticated organisation and manipulation could go hand-in-hand with a philosophical innocence. Once more we come to the impasse. It would seem that until we have really detailed studies of the 'blacke walkers in Westminster Hall', as Dering himself called them, we cannot discount Dering's hypothesis. This is too gloomy a conclusion. By a freak, much of Dering's correspondence at this crucial period has survived. It is possible to check Dering's public statements against his private views: some fascinating gaps appear.

When Dering wrote his apology in 1642, one of the ugliest episodes that he had to explain away was his presentation of a petition against episcopacy from Thomas Wilson on 10 November 1640. Wilson was to emerge as one of the most extreme 'root and branch' advocates. Dering, however, seized on the fact that Wilson *was to emerge* as a militant to argue that, in these salad days, Wilson *had not yet emerged* as such.[31]

Now Wilson was one of a number of correspondents who urged a zealous policy on Dering in the early months of 1641. The impression which these letters give is that they were directed to securing him to radical policies through emphasis upon zeal. William Barrett, writing in November 1640, called for 'zeale, courage and boldness for God and his truth' from Dering. His further remarks indicated that this meant more than generalised cant:

... that so your friends that have ingaged their Creditt for your faithfulness may have just cause to blesse God for you, and that those that are not as yet persuaded of your sincerity may be of another mind.[32]

In other letters of this period the same note is struck by writers to Dering: uncertainty about his position in religious matters; praise in the county for his actions in 1640; emphasis on the need for him to continue zealously until a radical reconstruction had taken place. In a letter of February 1641 – that is to say, three months before issues were clarified, according to Dering's public version of events – Wilson made clear to Dering what his supporters expected from his zeal in religious matters:

> Let the zeale of God's glory and his house eat you up. ... The way of other churches is to be minded and gone in [to].[33]

Two months later – still more than a month *before* the Root and Branch Bill – Wilson preached to the Commons. His sermon may be interpreted as a public extension of the point that he had made privately to Dering. This impression is reinforced by its public dedication to Dering, who is praised for his patronage of the zealous. Wilson contrasts their position with that of their opponents:

> they be professedly the children of the luke-warm, who say We will be no better than our Fathers.

Dering's zeal is of strategic importance, because 'Your present employment in the honourable House of Commons in Parliament calls for zeale'. The theocratic temper of the zealous comes out strongly in Wilson's words:

> A pious man's greatest care is that ... vile persons that speake villany, may have their mouthes stopped ... that the purity of discipline, very necessary to the condition of the Church, may be introduced.

Wilson – like Burges and Marshall in their sermons – presses for a complete reform according to the Will of God and warns against any acceptance of half-measures. The antithesis to zeal is luke-warmness. Lukewarmness, not zeal, provokes disorder. Zeal encourages eccentricity? Yes, but eccentricity is the mark of the puritan rejection of worldly worms:

> till a man seeme odd to the world, he is never right in religion and righteousnesse.

Zeal is primarily displayed in the search for God's sanction, and the rooting out completely of anything which lacks such sanction. He stresses that any project of a 'reduced' episcopacy, for instance, would be futile when once it had been demonstrated that it had no *iure divino* sanction:

> O think it not enough to clip their wings, when Christ is against the being of such a body.

Wilson makes clear his own partiality for a strict Presbyterian solution:

> Will not the beauty of the assemblies, a godly Ministery, a pure Discipline, a spirituall worship, bring in unto you much peace and comfort.[34]

Dering was arguing in his apology that the radicalism of his colleagues was not explicit until May 1641, when it forced him to affirm openly the moderate position that he had never really deserted. He claimed that his speeches in Parliament, his work on the Grand Committee of Religion, and even his presentation of the Kent petition for 'root and branch' of 13 January 1641 were as innocent of radicalism as his presentation of Wilson's petition had been two months earlier. More candid than he was with Wilson's petition, Dering acknowledged that the Kent petition was 'a Spawne of the London petition', but claimed that the qualifications which had been made to it robbed it of radical implications.[35]

While Dering was seeking, in his public apology, to show how it was possible, in the early months of 1641, to press zealously for reformation without compromising one's beliefs in a moderate episcopacy, an entirely contradictory picture was emerging from his private correspondence of that time. Most important was a letter from a local Anglican minister, Robert Abbott, to Dering on 15 March 1641.[36] It shows that, even at that early date, an advocate of a reformed, moderate episcopacy could be claimed at the extent to which Dering had encouraged ecclesiastical radicalism by his association with local ministers such as Wilson and Robson. On this view, any qualifications made to the Kent petition were trivial compared to the doctrines that were left standing:

> Be it therefore humbly and earnestly prayed, that this Hierarchicall power may be totally abrogated, if the wisdome of the Honourable House shall finde that it cannot be maintained by Gods Word and to his glory.[37]

Significantly, the Parliamentary diarist, Simonds D'Ewes, saw Dering's petition as no contribution to moderation. He described its aim as 'the ease and deliverance from the tyrannical power of the Bishops *and the abolishing of the verie hierachie it selfe*'.[38] Abbott makes clear, in his letter to Dering, that this is the logical inference to draw.

His letter opens with an acknowledgement that Dering's praises were ringing throughout the county as a good patriot of church and commonweath. Yet he implies that such fame may be spurious:

> ... yet hath not your worship beene free from default as well as meaner men.

Dering's major fault had been the encouragement which he has given to 'Brownists', who were growing, he claims, not only in Kent but in the country generally. At first 'it was thought that the high courses of some Bishops were the cause of their revolt from us: yet now they professe that Weare Bishops removed, the common prayer book and Ceremonies taken away, they would not join with us in Comunion. They stick not onely at our Bishops, service and Ceremonie, but at our church.' Abbott is concerned at the increasing number of men who pride themselves on their total rejection of episcopacy. He claims that Dering cannot altogether escape censure for this increase, since unwittingly he has played into the hands of these violent men:

> There are some things which they (together with some other well-affected people) have catcht at in your worships ... speech

and some other conference which they make the matter of pleasing discourse.

Abbott does not rest on generalities, but goes on to name the specific points, acceptable to the radicals, of which Dering had seemed to approve. It is worth noting that Abbott is not accusing Dering of favouring the 'Brownist' (or separatist) viewpoint, or indeed that of the Presbyterians. More subtly, he is saying that Dering's approval of certain principles fortified *either* movement.

First, on the localisation of the field of conflict: Dering had supported the thesis that episcopacy, 'as of foul breath', must be totally destroyed because it was totally corrupt. Abbott concedes that many disorders in the Church cry out for reform, yet he asks whether Dering meant his strictures to apply to the able preachers *within* the Church. He denounces as uncharitable his opponents' belief that 'among the Bishops, not one is better than another', and, while freely acknowledging faults in individuals, he points out that it is illogical to argue from the faults of the person to that of his office.

Second, Dering had encouraged those who wanted the people to have a say in the election of preachers. From his argument against the power of Canons and Synods to bind people without their assent, these people had gone on to say that 'surely it weare very unwright' if the people should have no share in the nomination of their minister. As a result, says Abbott, preachers not of the popular way have fallen into disrepute.

The third point is related to this: Dering has endangered the social structure by allying with those who have relied upon petitions. Another letter to Dering, written on the same day as Abbott's, was concerned solely with this point. The writer, one John Davies, who described himself as a 'Country Gentleman', showed a distaste for theological wranglings matched only by a concern about possible social convulsions. He deplored 'the Monstrous Easye Receit of Petitions' and the breakdown of the social hierarchy which it threatened. He somewhat invidiously singled out for praise 'your Sussex Neighbour, Mr. Justice Foster' for his work and said 'God send us more such to make up the breach'.[39] The point could hardly be lost on a man like Dering, whose prefatory note to his official apology of 1642 contains this gem:

> A well-fare to my reader, if hee be either of birth or breeding: A farewell to the rest.[40]

Abbott was also complaining that Dering's encouragement of petitions against ministers had awakened radical hopes. He pointed out that

> Richard Robson spake confidently unto mee, that your worship told him, if a Petition were drawn up agaynst a minister, and subscribed with 3 or 4 honest mans hands in the affirmative a thousand hands in the negative should doe him noe good.[41]

On those criteria there would be few Anglican ministers left: Abbott hoped that he had been misinformed.

Fourth, Dering had failed to put the case for a moderate episcopacy. While Dering had been right to attack clerical excesses, he should at the same time have made it clear that 'Episcopacy is lawful and a better way to governe the Church then any other that I know'. Abbott contrasted the Church of England with its Scottish neighbour:

> I look at the Church of Scotland which hath schooles, universities, and churches as well as we and I would faine see what learned men it hath trayned up in this last century to doe service against the Papal Church and Schoole of Arminius, answerable to the service of our Bishops.

He finds little in divinity to pit against 'that service which hath been done by our bishops and Episcopal men. Let the admired man in the world Archbishop Usher, Bishop Jewel, Bishop Morton, Bishop Abbott, Bishop Davenant, Bishop White, B. Downame, Dr. Willett, Dr. Mason in late times . . . witnesse plentifully.' These men were the masters in apologetics, because the fruits of episcopacy provided an incentive to study, although they did not study because of that incentive. If it is objected that not many nowadays have followed their inspired lead, Abbott's remedy is

to 'make this order lesse secular and more ecclesiasticall'. He
warns, above all, of the need to keep two things quite distinct:

> first a reformation in things truely amisse but not a ruine of
> right reverent order.

This should be accompanied by an attack on these 'who on a
pretext of attacking bishops have sought to overthrow the church.'
Abbott ends on virtually a threat:

> If I have misinterpreted your worships speech, I humbly
> submit and crave pardon . . . onlly be pleased to leave that be-
> cause I and all my friends are engaged in our votes for your
> worship, I could not but intimate my heart unto you this
> once.[42]

Abbott's arguments are interesting, not only as a good example
of the non-Laudian case for Anglicanism that was made in 1641
but also because of their influence upon Dering's subsequent behaviour. Dering's eyes were opened, not in May 1641 by a
dramatic change in the nature of radical protest but in March
1641 by an Anglican Father Joseph. By June 1641 Dering was
persuaded of the dangers of being identified with the party for
'ruin'. The basis for this hypothesis is not only contemporaries'
estimates of Abbott's influence,[43] somewhat complacently
acknowledged by Abbott himself in July 1641,[44] but also the
remarkable way in which Dering's volte-face of June 1641 follows
the lines which Abbott had laid down.

In his speech of 21 June 1641 Dering borrows from Abbott
the distinction between 'reform' and 'ruin'. By this time, he
argues, there are these two clear groupings in the Commons;
for this reason, he regards Vane's amendment, putting Church
government into the hands of lay commissioners, as 'an interregnum'. He does not attack the settlement as such, but rather
that it represents an evasion of the need for a settlement. He regards the scheme as a delaying device used by men who are looking to bolder, divinely sanctioned schemes, but who find it
difficult to proceed in the face of the king's fidelity to a reformed
episcopacy and antipathy to rival forms of government. Dering
stresses the importance of royal sanction and defends his model

of a 'primitive Episcopacy' on the grounds that it is at least a sincere attempt to provide government. Only a reduced episcopacy, in the form that he suggested, would be acceptable to King and Lords.[45]

Dering also borrowed from Abbott the argument about bishops' contribution to learning. He stressed the importance of apologetics:

> It is one thing to be able to preach and to fill the Pulpit well; it is another ability to confute the perverse adversaries of Truth and to stand in that breach.

Hence the need to cultivate the *rarae aves*: he stressed the contribution of bishops such as Jewel, Usher and Morton. They deserved to be rewarded for their services to learning: an argument which opponents of episcopacy ignore. Dering also criticised the assumption that all bishops had been at fault. The Laudians' offence belonged to their persons, not their office. There were many good bishops such as Williams, Morton, Hall (a curious time-lag this: Hall presumably won his place as the Calvinist of the thirties, not as the High Churchman of the forties), Curll, Potter and Duppa:

> Let us not make the day blacker in report than it is.[46]

Abbott had written to Dering of his distaste for the *iure divino* claims, from whatever quarter they came:

> It grieves me to reade upon every poste. The ordinance of Christ, the settled way of Christs Kingdom. Whether Episcopacy, Presbytery or Independent, congregations all doe plead under that title.[47]

Dering now argued that there were three possible opinions about episcopacy: that its sanction was *divinus, humanus* or *satanicus*. The first claim had been made by Hall; the third by his 'Antipent-agonists' (Hall's five opponents who wrote under the collective name 'Smectymnuus'); yet the second title was the valid one:

> it stands on good grounds, and pleads its own right by a good title.

The *iure divino* claim for episcopacy is an attempt to search for gold at a time when iron is only available usually; Dering counsels men to rest content with the silver of the *iure humano* claim. The tragedy is that half-measures will not placate the extremists, who seek for 'real gold', and 'with pressing for Ruine have betrayed the time of a blessed Reforming'. His impatience with the zeal of such men comes out in the words:

> And you that might have had enough, doe still cry more, more. To reform Episcopacy, it is in your esteem too faint, too cold a work ... to labour in the dressing and pruning of that plant which ... is not of God, and must be digged up.

He attacks an opponent:

> Learn moderation ... unlesse (as some of your Rooters doe seem to hold) you doe think moderation it selfe a vice.[48]

This illustrates how far he had travelled from the position which he had claimed for himself, at the beginning of his apology, as the constant champion of zeal.[49] Dering was trying to show that it was only after the debate on 'root and branch' in mid-1641 that it became impossible to press zealously for whole-hearted reform without commitment to a radical ecclesiastical programme; this was essential to his thesis that the change had taken place in his opponents, not in himself. Abbott's correspondence with Dering had shown that this was not true, even for the earlier period from November 1640 to May 1641: he revealed to Dering the alarming effects, in his own county, of his repudiation of moderation, and pointed the way to his later change of attitude.

But note that he did so, not by claiming that Dering was committed to Presbyterianism or Independency. Wilson was a Presbyterian; Robson probably was an Independent. No matter: the damage that Dering had done was by patronising these men by following certain lines of argument. Patronage could take place without commitment: that was the lesson that Dering echoed when he saw the dangers of a 'godly' solution that owed nothing to the numerical strength of Presbyterianism or Independency.

No lines of argument – it is evident not merely from this

correspondence but also from the great floods of pamphlets written at this time – did more to advance the prospects of a 'godly' solution than those which emphasised the total guilt of bishops (Marian martyrs included); the irrelevance of the support of the civil magistrate (arguments inflating the Emperor Constantine and *iure humano* justification for episcopacy were equally soundly trounced); the coming downfall of Antichrist; the prospects of a swift, total reformation; the need for zeal. All these are bound up with the apocalyptic prophecies of Thomas Brightman. Once we realise this, we are in a better position to do justice to the English Puritanism of 1641. All that neurotic harping on the need for zeal – echoed in Dering's correspondence, the 'root and branch' sermons of the period, and the pamphlets of Burges, Milton and Wilkinson [50] – falls into place when one realises that Brightman had offered as his key to the interpretation of the Book of Revelation the identification of Philadelphia, the zealous, with the Genevan and Scottish Churches. Conversely, Laodicea, the lukewarm, was identified with the Church of England:

> Both they and their whole luke-warm Hierarchie should quite be overthrown, and never recover their dignity againe.

When English Puritans extol zeal this is not empty bluster: a proof that they did not really know what to do until the Scots came along to tell them. On the contrary, when ministers spoke of zeal they knew that they were touching an eschatological nerve in their audience. And the mystery about the contradiction between the London ministers' messianic language in 1641 and their reverent tone to the magistrate before 1641 is likewise resolved. No need to assume that their royalism was faked *before* 1641 or – as Mrs Kirby somewhat desperately argues – that their royalism was not discarded *in* 1641. Neither is true: what needs to be remembered is that the Puritans' royalism before 1641 *was* messianic. Foxe had created for Puritans an idealised figure of the Godly Prince: the second Emperor Constantine. But Charles I was not Constantine, and Laud was not Cranmer. As faith in Crown and bishop receded, faith in the 'Godly Rule' that both were to create advanced. Puritans turned more and more to Brightman's vision of a reformation that would come, via neither Crown nor Bishop, but via a 'Godly People'. The jump in English Nonconformity from Foxe to Brightman was not the Great Leap Forward that W. A. Shaw had imagined: it was rather a tiny shuffle forward, although a most important shuffle. Centrifugal millenarianism replaced centripetal millenarianism.

In 1648 Benjamin Hubbard spoke of 'the prophet of this Centurie, the bright burning light of our age Master Thomas Brightman'.[51] The words were excessive; yet his influence on the 'root and branch' Puritans of the early 1640s *was* immense. When one sees the monolithic campaign in the literature of the time to debunk the Emperor Constantine, Queen Elizabeth, Cranmer, Latimer, Ridley and all the Foxe heroes; to stress the imminent founding of the New Jerusalem in the last Age of the World; to proclaim the importance of zeal; to attack all bishops as agents of Antichrist: it is hard to resist the suspicion that one follower of Brightman is masterminding a campaign in the way that Samuel Butler correctly saw London organising all those 'root and branch' petitions from different parts of England:

> The Parliament drew up petitions
> To itself, and sent them, like commissions,
> To well-affected persons, down
> In every city and great town,
> With pow'r to levy horse and men,
> Only to bring them back again.[52]

But this is almost certainly wrong. What we must instead emphasise is how men, brought up on the apocalyptic truths of Foxe, would naturally turn, in their disenchantment with Godly Prince and Godly Bishop, to the rival apocalyptic prophecies of Brightman. And – incensed at what would seem to them a mere deathbed repentance of Anglicanism – they would seek to destroy their opponents' new-found faith in the merits of the Elizabethan episcopacy, the Emperor Constantine and even the martyr-bishops.

It is the debt of English Puritanism to Brightman in 1641 that explains both its fervour and its seeming imprecision. On one point emphatically were ministers and pamphleteers precise: reform would *not* come via Godly Emperor or martyr-bishops. And Nathaniel Holmes is typical of many London ministers in 1641 in offering no hope for a Presbyterian theocracy either. Yet reform would come! The tone of the sermon was bracingly optimistic. Why, it was entitled 'The New Jerusalem'. His description of it is lifted bodily from the pages of Brightman's interpretation of the Book of Revelation. He did not explain very clearly how the 'New Jerusalem' would be built, but his audience in the Commons were left in no doubt that the destruction of the Whore of Babylon was imminent. Ministers such as Holmes were offering an uncompromising rejection of lukewarm episcopacy with no corresponding adherence to a specific alternative. Vines in 1656 pointed out that Brightman had rejected episcopacy as 'loathsome' but that he did not go so far as to advocate separatism. Canne argued that the one must follow from the other, while Ball – believing that Brightman was 'consonant to the non-conformists principles' – argued the contrary.[53] The point was that, in the period around 1641, separatist and non-separatist could join in approval of Brightman's rejection of a totally corrupt, lukewarm episcopacy.[54] The Scot, Robert Baillie, could approve of the radicalism of the London ministers and pamphleteers; they were emancipating themselves from Foxe. 'Root and Branch' was better than 'reduced episcopacy'; Brightman was better than Foxe.

But how much better? One crucial weakness remained. English Puritans continued to look to the Book of Revelation, not to the Presbyterian Book of Discipline, as the source of their inspiration. Brightman – as we have seen – came up with different answers from Foxe, *but they were different answers to the same question*. Later Baillie would deplore in his journal the extent to which apocalyptic interpretations went on influencing 'the most of the chief divines here, not only independents but others, such as Twis, Marshall, Palmer and many more'.[55] The ministers whom he named roared loudest for 'root and branch' destruction of episcopacy. They were less helpful with alternative proposals. This did not surprise Baillie. The Book of Revelation foretold in vivid and exciting language the downfall of Antichrist. What it did not do was the only thing that a Presbyterian minister cared about: mark out a Presbyterian discipline as the agent of that downfall.

Meantime the *prospect* of the downfall of Antichrist excited those who were later to differ about the *method* of its achievement. The Anglican, Edward Symmons, was curious how men had the nerve to take up arms against their sovereign. When a group of Roundheads were captured at Shrewsbury, he had a unique opportunity to discover the answer. They told him:

> 'tis prophesied in the Revelation, that the Whore of Babylon shall be destroyed with fire and sword, and what doe you know, but this is the time of her ruine, and that we are the men that must help to pull her down.[56]

There may be something almost comical about the spectacle of a contemporary mathematician of the stature of Napier valuing logarithms as a short cut to calculating the Number of the Beast. The example has been cited as a warning against exaggerating the modernity of the seventeenth-century scientist.[57] It is no less a warning against exaggerating the *esoteric* nature of such speculations. Millenarianism was more than a creed for cranks. The Book of Revelation is too often identified exclusively with sects such as the Fifth Monarchy Men in the 1650s. But we have seen that it also comforted the 'Monarchy' men in the 1630s: and now the 'No-Monarchy' men in the 1640s. The pursuit of the millennium was a *cause* as well as a *consequence* of the English Civil War.

When the ministers produced their extremely important apology, *Scripture and Reason Pleaded for Defensive Armes,* they denied that Parliament began the war with aggressive aims against bishops, but warned Royalists in 1643:

> Let them remember Mr. Brightmans Propheticall Interpretation of the spewing out of the Laodicean Angell.[58]

Something of that apocalyptic craving for a moral reform – what one minister, Fairclough, called a 'reall' reformation – was expressed by Thomas Case:

Oh if it might be reported in heaven that England is reformed – that such a drunkard, such a swearer, such a covetous
man . . . is become a new man.[59]

The 'Godly Rule' that men had once sought from 'royal' hands
was to be achieved by a 'real' reformation.

Baxter's cool comment in 1673 that 'Hookers principles begun
our warres' is misleading because it underrates the messianic
fervour generated by the 'root and branch' ministers in their
craving to establish a 'Godly Rule'.[60] More honest was his comment, in his autobiography, on what had made him side with
Parliament:

And I freely confess that, being astonished at the Irish
massacre, and persuaded fully both of the parliament's good
endeavours for reformation and of their real danger, my judgment of the main cause much swayed my judgment in the
matter of the wars. . . . And the consideration of the quality of
the parties that sided for each cause in the countries did greatly
work with me, and more than it should have done.[61]

If we see the Civil War only as the product of Hooker's principles,
or see in the sermons of the Puritan ministers only 'the dependence of the forces of righteousness upon Parliament', we are in
no position to understand the mentality of the men who burned
witches. Yet that is the other side of the 'Godly Rule' coin: an
expression of the same messianic conviction of the need to
purify. A pamphlet in 1646 described the burning of eighteen
witches in Suffolk. Bad beer brought Thomas Everard and his
wife to destruction:

Thomas Everard a Cooper, and Mary his wife, both being
imployed in a Brewhouse at Halsworth in the County of
Suffolke, freely confessed that they had bewitched Beere in
that Brewhouse; and that the odiousnesse of the infectious
stinke of it was such and so intollerable that . . . many people
dyed.

Civil war was a tiresome irrelevancy to the serious business of
witch-hunting:

Besides there are 120 more suspected Witches in prison, at
St. Edmunds-bury, who had all their Tryall now: but that the

Judge and Justices were compelled to adjourn the said Sessions till another time by reason of the neere approaching of the Cavaliers.

The search was admirably thorough:

There are in the County of Suffolke foure searchers appointed for the finding of them out, two men searchers and two women searchers, the men are to search those men who are suspected to be Witches, and the women searchers likewise are to search those women that are supposed to be witches. And also their maner is, in that Town so ever in the said County of Suffolke, there be any person or persons suspected to bewitch . . . thither they send for two or all of the said searchers, who take the partie or parties, so suspected into a Roome and strip him, her or them starke naked, and on whom the searchers find any teats or dugs, that partie or parties, the said searchers sit upon a stoole or stooles, in the midst of the Roome, so that the feete of him, her, or them, may not touch the ground . . . and in that time (if they be witches) either their Impes will come to suck him, her, or them, or else the partie or parties that is a Witch or Witches will be mightily perplexed and much tortured for want of his, her, or their sucking Impes, and will be strangely out of order, and fome at mouth, or else be in some other extraordinary seeming tormented posture, and many times they do apparently see their Impes come to them.[62]

It has been argued that the witchcraft delusion has often been disproportionately emphasised in Puritan history: that it played a small part in affairs and was soon over.[63] Yet it was no accident that the witch-hunting of the late 1640s should follow the millenarian expectations of the early 1640s. We have seen that Nathaniel Holmes, more explicitly than other London ministers, brought out the debt of the 'root and branch' campaign to the arguments of Thomas Brightman. Holmes, a disciple of William Perkins, was 'inclined to see in the activities of the Devil a presage of the last days'; in 1650 his pamphlet was published: 'Daemonologie and Theologie. The first, the Malady . . . The Second, the Remedy.'[64] Professor Trevor-Roper has brought out well the link between demonology and theology:

The basic evidence of the kingdom of God had been supplied by Revelation. But the Father of Lies had not revealed himself so openly. To penetrate the secrets of his Kingdoms, it was therefore necessary to rely on indirect sources. These sources could only be captured members of the enemy intelligence service: in other words, confessing witches.[65]

Or to put it another way: after Thomas Brightman, Matthew Hopkins; after the Apocalypse-seeker, the Witch-finder.

1. Joseph Hall, *Episcopacy by Divine Right* ...; *A Humble Remonstrance* ... ; *A Defence of the Humble Remonstrance* ... (London, 1641).

2. Peter Heylyn, *The Historie of Episcopacie* ..., preface.

3. Sir Benjamin Rudyerd, *Speech* ... (London, 1641) p. 20.

4. John Milton, *Of Reformation* ... (London, 1641) pp. 7, 8, 12, 15, 73; William Prynne, *The Antipathie* ... (London, 1641) I pp. 132, 133, 147; Smectymnuus, *An Answer to a Booke entitled, An Humble Remonstrance* ... (London, 1641) p. 103; William Thomas, *Speech* ... (London, 1641) p. 19; Nathaniel Fiennes, *Speech* ... (London, 1641) p. 6.

5. *Parliamentary History of England,* ed. W. Cobbett (London, 1808) IV 153.

6. Roger L'Estrange, *The Relapsed Apostate* ... (London, 1661) p. 72.

7. Valerie Pearl, *London and the Outbreak of the Puritan Revolution* (Oxford University Press, 1961) pp 160–76.

8. J. H. Hexter, *The Reign of King Pym* (Cambridge, Massachusetts, 1941) *passim.*

9. W. A. Shaw, *A History of the English Church, 1640–1660* (London, Longmans, 1900) I 7, 316.

10. William Bridge, *Babylon's Downfall* (London, 1641); Cornelius Burges, *The First Sermon* ... (London, 1641); E. W. Kirby, 'Sermons Before the Commons, 1640–2' *American Historical Review,* XLIV (1938–9) 528–48.

11. Robert Baillie, *Letters and Journals* ..., ed. D. Laing (Edinburgh, 1841) II 220–1.

12. Nathaniel Hardy, *The Arraignment of Licentious Libertie* ... (London, 1647) dedicatory epistle.

13. Thomas Coleman, *Maledicis* ... (London, 1646) pp. 36–9.

14. Historical Manuscripts Commission, *13th Report,* I 95.

15. Noted by John Saltmarsh in his *Some Drops of the Viall* ... (London, 1646) VII 22.

16. Sir Edward Dering, *Collection of Speeches* ... (London, 1642) p. 3.

17. Stephen Marshall, *A Sermon* ... (London, 1641) p. 47; Thomas Case, *The Second Sermon* ... (London, 1641) p. 36; Thomas Goodwin, *Zerrubabels Encouragement* ... (London, 1642) p. 52; Edmund Calamy, *God's Free Mercy to England* (London, 1641) p. 12; Stephen Marshall, *A Peace-Offering to God* (London, 1641) p. 37.

18. (Doctor Williams's Library) Baxter MSS. 59.2, f. 218v.

19. (Doctor Williams's Library) Baxter MSS. 59.3, f. 80. Burges said to Baxter that he, White, Marshall, Calamy and one or two other ministers used to meet twice a week in one of their lodgings. Also present at these meetings were Warwick, Hampden, Pym and others, 'and not one was for totall abolishing of all, or any, but usurped Episcopacy'.

20. Baillie, *Letters and Journals* ..., I 302–3; John Lightfoot, *Works* ... (London, 1823) XIII 11.

21. William Haller, 'John Foxe and the Puritan Revolution' in *The Seventeenth Century*, ed. R. F. Jones (Stamford University Press, 1951) p. 221.

22. Cornelius Burges, *The First Sermon* ..., p. 54.

23. See my 'Episcopacy and a "Godly Discipline", 1641–6', *Journal of Ecclesiastical History*, X 1 (April 1959) 74–89, for a detailed discussion of this division.

24. Sir Edward Dering, *Collection of Speeches* ..., p. 99.

25. Ibid., pp. 2, 4, 5. J. Bruce, in his Preface to *Proceedings* ... *in* ... *Kent* ..., ed. L. Larking (Camden Society, 1862) largely accepts Dering's account of his evolution.

26. Clarendon, *The History of the Rebellion* ... *in England* ..., ed. W. Macray (Oxford, 1888) I 314.

27. Clarendon, *Selections* ..., ed. G. Huehns (Oxford University Press, 1953) p. 26. Clarendon asked the 'root and branch' partisan, Nathaniel Fiennes, what he would have in place of episcopacy. Fiennes's reply (according to Clarendon) was that 'there would be time enough to think of that'.

28. Dering, *Collection of Speeches*, p. 2.

29. Peter Heylyn, *Cyprianus Anglicus*, pp. 538, 540; *A Briefe Relation* ... (Oxford, 1644) p. 27. Alan Everitt, *The Community of Kent and the Great Rebellion 1640–1660* (Leicester University Press, 1966) pp. 62–83, contains a masterly account of Dering's social environment and connections. He rightly argues that Dering was no Presbyterian and that his ideal form of

government would have been 'virtually autonomous county churches' (see details of Dering's reform plan: ibid., p. 53). Dr Everitt concedes, however (ibid., pp. 62–3), that Dering's 'academic detachment and impulsive, sympathetic nature laid him open to the eager influence of puritans like Thomas Wilson at home and Sir Henry Vane and Sir Arthur Hesilrige in the House of Commons'. I propose to argue that this influence swung him off course in the early months of 1641 to a far greater extent than he was prepared to acknowledge in his memoirs, and that he was brought back *on* course only by the most spirited counterpressure of Robert Abbott.

30. Dering, *Collection of Speeches,* pp. 4–5.

31. Although Wilson had already fallen foul of Laud. Along with Richard Culmer, he had been suspended for refusing to read the Book of Sports. He 'continued to preach in his rectory in secret and on one occasion, when a pursuivant from the Council suddenly appeared, narrowly escaped arrest by slipping through a doorway in the screen at the back of the hall': Everitt, *The Community of Kent . . .,* p. 59. Heylyn, *Cyprianus Anglicus . . .,* p. 308, called Wilson, Culmer and Player the 'leading men, and the chief sticklers of the faction in all his Diocess'. For another view of Culmer, see *Calendar State Papers Domestic, Charles I,* CCCCLXXVI 454. Prynne, *Canterburies Doome . . .,* p. 149, called Wilson 'a godly learned Minister'.

32. *Proceedings in Kent . . .,* ed. L. Larking, p. 22.

33. Ibid., p. 23 (British Museum) Stowe MSS. 184, f. 10, f. 19. Richard Skeffington, urging on Dering the need for a total reconstruction, referred him to 'my dear Friende Mr. Pyme'.

34. Thomas Wilson, *Davids Zeale for Zion . . .* (London, 1641) dedicatory epistle, pp. 14, 15, 17, 28, 44.

35. Dering, *Collection of Speeches,* p. 17. For important evidence on the link between the London and Kent petitions, see *Proceedings in Kent . . .,* pp. 23–38; Robson: Dering, 1 December 1640. Dering pointed to the reduced length, more moderate language, and disavowal of the plea to numbers in the Kent petition: Dering, *Collection of Speeches,* p. 19.

36. (B.M.) Stowe MSS. 184, f. 27–f. 29.

37. Dering, *Collection of Speeches,* p. 23.

38. Simonds D'Ewes, *Journal . . .,* ed. W. Notestein (London, O.U.P., 1924) I 249. My italics.

39. (B.M.) Stowe MSS. 184, f. 27, f. 27v, f. 31.

40. Dering, *Collection of Speeches,* dedicatory epistle.

41. (B.M.) Stowe MSS. 184, f. 27v–f. 28. For evidence of the

link between Dering and Robson, see: *Proceedings in Kent . . .*, ed. L. Larking, pp. 25–8.

42. (B.M.) Stowe MSS. 184, f. 28v–f. 29.

43. Dering, *Collection of Speeches,* pp. 162–4.

44. (B.M.) Stowe MSS. 184, f. 43; Abbott: Dering: 'Now they say, that Sir Edward Dering, who fought in the front, wheeles about. You were pleased to give mee a touch, and thence I apprehend the ground.'

45. Dering, *Collection of Speeches,* pp. 66, 67, 68, 74. Dering had described (p. 77) the hostile reaction to his rival proposal of a 'moderate episcopacy' from the City and the ministers who, as he rightly points out, were for the most part 'absolutely anti-Episcopall'. Their lack of concern, on the other hand, about Vane's scheme of July 1641 – 'a standard of Anglican Puritanism essentially non-Presbyterian' (W. A. Shaw, *A History of the English Church, 1604–1660* I 100) – supports Dering's belief that the triumph of Vane's plan was thought unlikely in the Commons then. On the other hand, in 1645, when we shall see that Erastian sentiments were prevailing in the Commons, Vane's scheme was hailed as proof of the Commons' consistency. This was the position argued by the leading Erastian, Thomas Coleman: *A Brotherly Examination Re-Examined . . .* (London, 1645) p. 10. W. A. Shaw, *History of the English Church,* I 98, took over Coleman's position to argue that, therefore, 'throughout this course of mental evolution the Parliament was thoroughly true to the national instinct, and would have remained so had it not been that the course of the war made it necessary to accept Scotch aid at the price of the adoption of the Scottish Church system'. This is to place altogether too low an emphasis on the clericalist sentiments of native ministers – and upon their influence on the Commons – before the coming of the Scots. As John Ley pointed out, in reply to Coleman, the scheme had ultimately failed to go through Parliament, not because of the intrigues of a few, but for a reason that few Erastians of 1645 cared to acknowledge: namely its lack of appeal to those who were thirsting for a 'real' reformation (and they then *included* Coleman) – 'Because the Interimisticall Magistracie, that was projected was too like Prelacie to be liked (by such as desired a thorow Reformation) and that in three things especially. 1. In that it had no warrant in the word of God. 2. That it would shrinke up the power into a few hands, which should be communicated to many, as the Prelacie did. 3. In that it was contrary to the example of all the truly reformed Churches in the Christian World': John Ley, *The New Querie . . .* (London, 1645) p. 52. In the next chapter we shall try to understand

why to Erastians such as Coleman and Prynne these objections should seem trifling in 1645 and yet insuperable in 1641. Naturally Coleman would seek to conceal this change, but our evidence supports Dering's contention that – in 1641 – this 'Interimisticall Magistracie' was not seen as a viable alternative to the total reformation sought by a 'Godly People'.

46. Dering, *Collection of Speeches,* pp. 112, 113.

47. (B.M.) Stowe MSS. 184, f. 33. Cf. (B.M.) Stowe MSS. 744, f. 12, for a similar reminder by Abbott to Dering of the folly of this claim.

48. Dering, *Collection of Speeches,* pp. 125, 130, 165.

49. Ibid., p. 2.

50. Cornelius Burges, *The First Sermon . . .;* John Milton, *Of Reformation . . .;* Henry Wilkinson, *A Sermon Against Luke-warmenesse in Religion* (London, 1640).

51. Benjamin Hubbard, *Sermo Saecularis* (London, 1648) p. 28. Two writers (E. Tuveson, *Millennium and Utopia* and M. Walzer, *Revolution of the Saints*) who have argued for the importance of millenarian thought in the Civil War would have put Joseph Mead's influence even higher than Thomas Brightman's. Mead is certainly an important influence on Civil War millenarianism. But Tuveson's reason for putting him higher than Brightman is the more optimistic and resilient note in the later writer (Tuveson, op. cit., pp. 79–80). Walzer (op. cit., p. 292) disagrees and shows how much of Brightman is in Mead. If he too, in the end, underrates Brightman it may be because he has missed the significance of Brightman's challenge to Foxe. We have already seen that Foxe is the blind spot in Walzer's valuable study.

52. Samuel Butler, *Hudibras,* II 609–14.

53. Richard Vines, *A Treatise . . .* (London, 1656) p. 242; John Canne, *A Necessity of Separation . . .* (London, 1654) pp. 18–21; John Ball, *An Answer . . .* (London, 1642) p. 33.

54. The Presbyterian Thomas Edwards in his *Gangraena . . .* III, dedicatory epistle, mentions how his exposition of Brightman's interpretation of Revelation in a lecture in 1638 had found favour with the separatist, John Goodwin.

55. Baillie, *Letters and Journals . . .* II 313.

56. Edward Symmons, *Scripture Vindicated . . .* (Oxford, 1645) preface.

57. H. F. Kearney, 'Puritanism, Capitalism and the Scientific Revolution', *Past and Present* 28, p. 88.

58. *Scripture and Reason Pleaded for Defensive Armes . . .*

by divers Reverend and Learned Divines . . . (London, 1643) p. 66.

59. Samuel Fairclough, *The Troublers Troubled . . .* (London, 1641) p. 30; Thomas Case, *The Second Sermon . . .* p. 47.

60. Michael Walzer, *The Revolution of the Saints*, p. 4, is good on this kind of myopia. Baxter is falling here into the Clarendon trap – of failing to grasp the arrival of 'the active, ideologically committed political radical'; of dismissing the Puritan Revolution as a *Fronde*.

61. Richard Baxter, *Autobiography*, p. 36.

62. (Anon.), *True Relation of the Araignment of Eighteene Witches . . .* (London, 1646) pp. 1, 5, 6.

63. P. Miller and T. Johnson, eds., *The Puritans* (Harper Torchbooks, 1963), p. 804.

64. W. Notestein, *A History of Witchcraft in England from 1558 to 1718* (New York, 1956) p. 240.

65. H. R. Trevor-Roper, 'Witches and Witchcraft', *Encounter* (May 1967) p. 15.

5 Godly Parliament

Millenarianism seems to be at a peak in the late 1640s and throughout the 1650s. This is the time, above all, when the activities of groups such as the Fifth Monarchy Men and Ranters pose the most serious threat to political stability. But, on the argument that has been developed so far, this should be taken as a symptom of the *decline*, not the *growth*, of the importance of millenarian thought in Protestant England. For we have seen that the achievement of millenarian interpreters such as Brightman and Foxe was to canalise apocalyptic enthusiasm in two important ways: to encourage belief in the imminent downfall of Antichrist without naming the day[1] and to encourage individual zeal without destroying belief in established institutions (Godly Prince or Godly Ministry). Neither proposition holds true of the radical sects in the middle of the seventeenth century who dated the precise time of the downfall of Antichrist with a confidence that would have dismayed Foxe or Brightman, and who repudiated the traditional organs of authority. There was obviously much greater potential for subversion in Brightman than in Foxe; he had, after all, already voted no confidence in prince or bishop. But at least he had expressed his faith in the Godly People: the inspired ministers of the Gospel who would chart the New Jerusalem. Before the extremist views of sects such as the Fifth Monarchy Men could prevail, the 'root and branch' ministers had to demonstrate their incapacity to fulfil Brightman's hopes in the same way that Charles I had revealed himself incapable of playing the Emperor Constantine. The ministers largely destroyed this trust in some vicious in-fighting over the Sacrament of the Lord's Supper, although it is fair to say that some of this arose because they had already destroyed this trust. Millenarianism shrank from being the property of the nation to being the property of a party when it fell into the hands of those who rejected the mediation of king, bishop or prince. And this tendency was fortified by a circular process: the more that millenarianism became associated with political and social extremism, the more *former* millenarians would be anxious to play down the extent of earlier commitments. Stephen Marshall could argue in 1643:

> Yet time (one of the best Interpreters of Prophecies) hath produced the events answering the types so full and clear; that we have the whole Army of Protestant Interpreters agreeing on the generall scope and meaning of it.[2]

This claim was dubious even in 1643, although at the time when the New Model Army seemed to be about to fashion a 'Godly Rule' it carried a plausibility that it demonstrably lacked a decade or so later when it was seen that the Civil War had spawned so many conflicting and eccentric interpretations of the Apocalypse.

When did Marshall's consensus break down? We have seen that, as early as 1641, the 'root and branch' campaign cloaked, by its very success, a real ambiguity in Brightman's thesis. Was he arguing *for* a Presbyterian hierarchy, or *for* a congregational separatism, when he argued *against* bishops? The controversy over admission to the Sacrament of the Lord's Supper underlined the ambiguity, discredited Brightman's 'Godly People', and in the end destroyed the whole concept of 'Godly Rule'. But only in the end: there are two stages in this controversy and they will be discussed in these next two chapters.

The first stage of the controversy is in the late 1640s; the second stage is in the Protectorate. Superficially they seem very similar. Many of the arguments of the 1640s will be repeated in the 1650s; many of the protagonists in these controveries will be the same. But there is one vital difference. In the 1640s both parties to the dispute could look to a Parliament or to a Westminster Assembly of Divines to carry out their proposals; in the 1650s both had to contend with Oliver Cromwell and with his highly personal definition of the functions of ruling. The controversy over administering the Sacrament of the Lord's Supper has never quite received the attention that it deserves. Thus a recent interesting study of English Presbyterianism can describe its collapse during the Interregnum almost entirely in *political* terms[3]: there is no hint that its *philosophical* foundations were shattered in the course of this controversy. Any idea that this controversy is of minor importance is most emphatically not borne out by a study of the pamphlet literature of the 1640s and 1650s.

One cannot understand the passions aroused by this issue unless one understands the tremendous feeling of disappointment that was rampant among English Puritans in 1645:

> But whence it is that Devils should choose to be conversant with silly Women who know not their right hands from their left, is the great wonder.... If the Devil be so wise, and wise to do evill, why should he not choose to deale with wise Men, and great Men?... than to attend old women, and kill Hens, Geese, Pigs, Hogs, Calves, and little children.[4]

Why indeed? And why – anxiously asked men in August 1645 – was the Devil still invincible in an England that had dedicated itself to his destruction? Among Puritans at this time there is much beating of breasts at the spectacle of moral depravity. One London minister, Palmer, remarked that 'above all former times, whoredom and adultery doe frequently abound and grow Impudent, even Incest is to be found in divers places, and no punishment to be found for it'.[5] We would now say that the Puritans caricatured their plight: if there was a breakdown of order, this was hardly surprising in the middle of a Civil War. But this is not to say that the laments were insincere. Rather, they have the preposterous sincerity of a jilted lover.

The disenchantment of 1645 can only be understood against the background of the inflated hopes of 1641. After all, in that year, we saw that a London minister such as Thomas Wilson had promised his audience in the Commons that 'vile persons that spake villany' would have 'their mouthes stopped'.[6] He was typical of his colleagues in the stress that he placed on the speed with which the cleansing operation would be carried out. In their sermons the ministers absurdly underrated the difficulties that attended a 'real' reformation. Fairclough, Case, Holmes, Symonds all stressed the importance of speed.[7] This won them an immediate tactical advantage over their Anglican rivals, who were preaching caution, deliberation, delay. Morley, for instance, put the Anglican case in 1641:

> That the reforming of abuses in Episcopall government will take a long time, that we are apt to believe; but we think this no objection ... it ought to be a businesse of much debate and deliberation: and that it imports not so much to be quickly done as well done.[8]

Nothing could be wiser, graver or more statesmanlike – and nothing less likely to excite men who had come to hear about the downfall of Antichrist! When by 1644 preachers such as Palmer and Hill – whose 'Scottish and free sermons' earlier had won the applause of Robert Baillie – borrowed from their Anglican opponents of 1641 arguments in favour of cautious advance, they were tacitly acknowledging their failure to implement the speedy reform that had been promised. At the same time they ruefully recognised the fillip that this failure had given to Erastianism *within their own ranks*. Hill desperately conceded that opinions 'of most dangerous consequence begin now to spring among us ... such who would have nothing *iure divino*, nothing stands by divine right in Church affaires, but resolve all wholly into State power and civill policy'.[9] And this was the time that the Presbyterian, Robert Baillie, also noted that a 'Civilian' group in the Commons had sprung up who were anxious that 'Erastus' way would triumph'.[10] This anxiety was expressed in hostility to the Westminster Assembly of Divines; above all, to the claim of ministers in the Assembly to a right, by divine warrant, to suspend unworthy persons from the Sacrament of the Lord's Supper.

If one regards the Covenant and the Westminster Assembly merely as the price that England paid in order to obtain military help from the Scots, it is easy to explain this Erastian revival after 1644. On this view, it was the natural response of men who were no longer obliged to toady to the Scots. But there had been nothing abject about the mood of 1643. Pym wanted a Scottish alliance; the Scots wanted a Covenant and an Assembly of Divines. But this did not mean that Vane, on behalf of the Commons, sold out to the Scots; indeed, we know now that his colleagues in the Commons went further even than he did in checking Scottish ambitions.[11] The Assembly – both in constitution and personnel – fell far short of Scottish desires. But to say that the Covenant and the Assembly were not a sell-out to Presbyterianism is *not* to say that they were not a sell-out to clericalism. This was immediately grasped by an anti-clerical lawyer such as Selden. He saw that a synod of divines – whatever limitations were hedged around it – was itself an affront to the State:

> To call so many Divines together will bee to putt power into their hands who are apt to usurpe it, as if the Laytye were bound by their determinacons.... If you would buy Gloves send for a Glover or two, not Glovers hall; Consult with some divines, not send for a body.[12]

Far from being cowed by Scottish pressure, Selden from the start led an implacable opposition to the Assembly. When Baillie complained in 1645 that 'Mr. Prin and the Erastian lawyers are now our *remora*',[13] he had in mind a different group from these persistent anti-clericalists. There is no mystery about Selden's opposition to clericalism in 1645; there is about some of the allies that he had recruited to his side by that date.

The mystery can be resolved if we realise the appeal of the Covenant and an Assembly to men fired by millenarian hopes. Time and time again the London ministers had pressed for both, but in the context of that speedy reformation that would destroy Antichrist. Failure to achieve that reformation cast serious doubt upon both. Once we had the Covenant, promised Burges in 1641[14] – and remember that this was no surrender to the Scots, and Burges would make clear his position on that in 1643[15] – the work of Reformation would go on 'merily' and men would prosper. A slow building, a 'heavy' Reformation, was a denial of a Covenant with God: a comment that would look sinister when the Westminster Assembly talked so much and achieved so little. Similarly, Burroughs in 1641 had pointed out that, while reckless speed had brought about Laud's downfall, the moral for 'root and branch' men was not to proceed cautiously. The difference between the two cases was that one had the approval of God:

> For though mens suddenesse often proves their ruine, yet what God does suddenly is done strongly and surely; Created things that are properly Gods are alwaies sudden.[16]

Always? What then of the Westminster Assembly? In what sense could it be representing the Will of God? No body sowed disenchantment so effectively as the Westminster Assembly. In one sense, the members deserve our sympathy. Their problem was to honour the promises made by the 'root and branch' ministers of 1641. The Apocalypse did not make for cool thinking. Consistently the London ministers had underrated the problems involved in fashioning a 'Godly Rule'. Once you ridded yourself of Antichrist, what then? As Baxter confessed to a friend, '20 most learned Expositions were in the hardest points often as not of 16 or 17 mindes'. Perhaps even this was an understatement. One most learned exposition – that of Brightman – kept men arguing for long enough by itself. The Westminster Assembly, set up during the Civil War to resolve such problems, predictably *became the arena in which they were discussed*. The Assembly won notoriety for its slowness. When the idea of a revived Assembly of Divines was floated in 1658, Baxter was crisply dismissive: 'they will doe less in a month than one or two men will doe in a day or two'. He knew.[17]

The Assembly's failure could be read two ways. It could be read by anti-clerical lawyers, such as John Selden, as an argument against the whole idea of a Godly Rule. It was. But it also could be read by some Erastians, such as Thomas Coleman, as an argument for distinguishing between *Godly* and *Clerical* Rule. Coleman would turn to Parliament to achieve this moral reform, the downfall of Antichrist, which the Assembly had promised to achieve but by 1645 patently had not achieved. It is important to see that despair at moral laxity in the late 1640s was usually linked with sharp comments about the progress of the Westminster Assembly. The feeling was summed up in the rebuke of *The Scottish Dove*:

> It were more Honourable to themselves (that are Divines) that have nothing but contentions to follow, to imploy themselves in the Northern parts, to reduce and convert those souls to God . . . there is want of good preachers.

Ministers such as Baillie, Henderson, Hill and Palmer recognised the truth of the observation: the failure of the Assembly to achieve rapid moral reform was leading men to look to other instruments for this purpose. If not the Assembly, why not the Parliament? This was not the motive behind Selden's stand, but Baillie in his acute comments at the time never held any illusions about *him*. The Assembly's efforts to set up a 'godly discipline' had not seriously been retarded by Erastian opposition; the major Erastian opposition had arisen *because* of the failure of the Assembly's efforts to set up a 'godly discipline'. As *The Scottish Dove* put it quite simply: Erastianism is 'an effect of Gods anger against the nation for non-reformation'. Why this non-reformation? The committed Presbyterian blamed primarily the Independents, although his attitude towards them fluctuated bewilderingly. In 1643 and early 1644 he was confident of establishing a Presbyterian National Church. But, as Baillie said, 'if we carry not the Independents with us, there will be ground laid for a very troublesome schism'. Hence the Presbyterian tactics with the Independents were 'not to meddle in haste'. The reward of patience would be reconciliation. All this seems fatuously naïve now; but not then, when the differences between the two had not become so pronounced. But already in early 1644 the Presbyterian could see that the bickering over minutiae in the Assembly was making impatient some of the English Puritans. This was the time when Baillie castigated chiliasm as the English disease: most of his 'root and branch' colleagues were 'expresse Chiliasts'. The millenarianism of a man such as Stephen Marshall had made him a welcome ally in 1641 to the Scottish Presbyterians when the enemy was Anglican compromise; a dubious ally by 1644 when *Presbyterian* compromise was demanded.[18] Feeling that the situation was slipping away from them, the Presbyterians vented their wrath on the Independents: the men whom they were coming to hold responsible for the slow progress in the Assembly. By the end of 1644, and 1645, the Presbyterian was determined to secure disciplinary control over offenders: preferably within the context of a National Presbyterian Church; if need be, without. When the second alternative became more likely, Presbyterians found themselves close to the position of many Independent ministers who were seeking similar powers. The Presbyterians' attitude to their Independent colleagues fall into three stages therefore: attempted negotiations; bitter recriminations; an accidental solidarity. These are very rough divisions for the period between 1643 and 1646; there are frequent overlaps and inconsistencies of behaviour. Nevertheless the usefulness of the distinction is this: if we assume a consistently malevolent or benevolent party line adopted by the Presbyterian ministers to the Independents, we miss the complexity of the controversies within these years. And – more crucial – we miss the significance of the Erastian response.

For the Erastian revival was prompted by two things: the failure of the Westminster Assembly to bring about the promised moral reform; the claims of the clergymen – Presbyterian *and* Independent – for more stringent disciplinary powers. To the Erastian, the two were connected. To Erastus himself, the two had been connected.

Erastianism is conventionally understood as the claim of the secular power to control belief; it carries with it pejorative connotations of a cynical indifference to moral questions. The figures whom it conjures to mind are a Selden and a Hobbes. As a description of Erastus's own position, this will not do. J. N. Figgis exposed this delusion some fifty years ago. Erastus had been concerned with the question of how to enforce ecclesiastical discipline in a State which was uniform in its religion: the limits of the magistrate's coercive authority and the rights of a persecuted minority to speak the truth were points not germane to this purpose. Erastus's discussion of excommunication was a rejoinder to the theses of George Wither, who in Heidelberg in 1568 had proclaimed a *iure divino* power for the clergy, in excommunicating and suspending those whom they judged to be unworthy to attend the Sacrament with them. Erastus sought to resist the imposition of the Genevan system upon Heidelberg: for him 'the main object was not to magnify the civil power, but to oppose the discipline'. Erastus's opposition was rooted in an ethical concern: 'it seemed to him highly inexpedient to set about excommunicating a population who in reality needed conversion'. Moreover, the clerical claim to judge the sincerity of the persistent offender seemed to Erastus a presumptuous encroachment upon God's Prerogative. In arguing against excommunication, Erastus incidentally advanced the proposition that the magistrate could implement the ethical reform, at which the clergy professedly aimed. Only in this oblique way did Erastus touch at all upon the authority of the civil magistrate, and even then he did not include within its bounds the power of excommunication or definition of faith: 'he is only considering the case where prince and people are all of the same religion and that the true one'. Figgis points out that Erastus was not blamed in his own day for giving too much power to the magistrate; divines, such as Bullinger, treated him as a much respected colleague; his refusal to serve under a Lutheran magistrate in 1576 is a mark of his distance from the popular concept of an Erastian. And, in that pejorative sense, the term only became popular in England in the mid-1640s. It was Scottish Presbyterians, such as Baillie, Gillespie and Rutherford, who first used the term emotively to discredit those who opposed the Westminster Assembly. Figgis believed that

> The extension of the term Erastian to mean not opponents of excommunication, but upholders of the view that the magistrate could order religion as he liked and command obedience, was due to this controversy.[19]

We must not be deceived by the propaganda of the Scottish ministers: they were not self-deceived. They might bluster about the Erastians' idolatry of the civil ruler, but they knew that the revival of Erastian sentiments had in fact been fostered *by reading Erastus*. They knew how telling his criticisms were at a time when clerics had failed to give a moral lead. They knew why the claims that they – and their Independent colleagues – were making for severer disciplinary powers should be particularly offensive to followers of Erastus. They knew the need to counter Erastus's arguments by equally patient scholarship: hence the formidably erudite works of Gillespie and Rutherford.[20] They knew that their most dangerous enemy was not a John Selden, whose ill-will they could count on, but a Thomas Coleman, Erastus's greatest disciple.

Thomas Coleman is a seriously undervalued figure; his role in the Erastian controversies is a crucial one. This Lincolnshire rector, nicknamed 'Rabbi Coleman' for his hebraist scholarship, became the scourge of the Scots. To one of them, George Gillespie, Erastianism was 'that pestilence that walketh in darknesse through London and Westminster'. In another pamphlet, Gillespie saw it as a dying body revived by a medical genius:

> But now, while Erastianism did thus lye a dying, and like to breathe its last, is there no Physitian who will undertake to cure, and endeavour to rise it up from the gates of death to life? Yes, Mr. Coleman was the man, who (to that purpose) first appeared publikely.[21]

Gillespie had no doubt that it was Coleman who had wrecked the chance of unity in the Westminster Assembly with his advocacy of 'Erastian Tenents'.[22] Baillie wrote to Dickson in March 1646 to complain about the influence that Coleman exercised upon the lawyers in the Commons: 'So he is become their champion, to bring out, in the best way he can Erastus's arguments'.[23] As Gillespie pointed out, one of Coleman's aims had been to translate, and publish in English, Erastus's writings against excommunication. By 1647, however, he was dead, and Gillespie chortled: 'The Lord was pleased to remove him by death, before he could do what he intended in this, and other particulars.' Baillie also derived grim satisfaction from Coleman's death. He wrote to Spang:

> God has struck Coleman with death; he fell on an ague and after 4 or 5 days expired. It is not good to stand in Christs way.[24]

Two other leading Erastian controversialists acknowledged their debt to Coleman.[25] The minister, Francis Woodcock, had the misfortune to preach a sermon on the same day as Coleman. Woodcock found his glory eclipsed:

> so much of novelty in it, and which so wholly took up the mindes of many, that till the wonder thereof was over, I despaired that any thing I could publish would be vouchsafed a look from them.[26]

What is striking in all this is not the agreement among friends and enemies about Coleman's importance in the Erastian controversies, but their agreement about *the way* in which he is important. He – and those like him – are different animals from the cynics. The 'Parliament-Pressing' Thomas Case extolled Coleman's 1643 sermon on the Covenant; Thomas Edwards, the apostle of Presbyterian intolerance, called Coleman an honoured colleague, who shared his concern at the moral abuses of the time; a moderate such as Featley bracketed him with the 'root and branch' men, whose pro-Scottish tendencies he deplored.[27] Thomas Fuller described Selden's obstructionist tactics against the Westminster Assembly, but in a separate paragraph referred to 'Mr. Thomas Coleman, a modest and learned man, beneficed in Lincolnshire, and Mr. John Lightfoot, well skilled in rabbinical learning, [who] were the chiefe members of the Assembly, who (for the main) maintained the tenets of Erastus'.[28] Similarly, an anonymous correspondent in a letter to Baxter distinguished men close to Erastus's views, such as Coleman, Lightfoot and Stillingfleet, from 'ill principled men such as Selden, Grotius and Hobbes, 'as bad as can be'.[29]

Ironically, Baxter himself, some ten years after Coleman's death, remembered him as the supporter of moderate episcopacy.[30] Although this was fair comment on Coleman's position in the Erastian controversy, it misread his attitude earlier. For once Coleman had been an enthusiast for the 'root and branch' destruction of episcopacy. In 1643 he had argued that the *moral* superiority of the Parliamentary side vindicated its cause. He rejoiced in the quality of the preachers:

Minde what kinde of Ministers flocke to us, and we receive
and provide for; With us are the Priests, the Ministers of the
Lord . . . such who have been diligent, and painfull in their
callings, zealous for the Lorde and his worke, desirous and
careful to have it done as He commands.[31]

To the anti-clerical cynic this stress on preaching would seem
fatuous. To Selden, preaching 'is the glory of the preacher to
shew him self a fine man'; Hobbes asked: 'What needs so much
preaching of faith to us that are not heathens?'[32]

Of episcopacy, Coleman said in 1643 – 'Up with it, up with
it to the bottome, root and branch.' He echoed the London
ministers' emphasis on speed:

> Cursed is he that doth the worke of the Lord negligently;
> The Enemy destroyes a Kingdome by doing, and a friend
> by not doing.[33]

In this context, the Covenant could be welcomed as an instrument of moral reform, binding together English and Scots:
'they shall have the same ministry and Religion.' What of the
objection to imposing an oath 'upon implicit faith'? Coleman
would have none of it – 'an impertinent scruple', was how he
dismissed it. What of the objection that Parliament might find
it convenient to restore episcopacy, and thus dishonour its
oath? Coleman would stomach no sophistries on that score:
episcopacy had to be totally removed. He denied that 'the most
wicked antichristian government' would ever be restored.

The language is highly revealing. William Prynne was to
join Coleman in his Erastian stand in 1645. But earlier he too
had been ready to denounce episcopacy as Antichristian. The
Independent, John Goodwin, saw a contradiction in the two
positions:

> if no prescript forme in the Worde, why not Episcopacie as
> well as Presbyterie? Why such crying down of Bishops as
> Anti-Christian, for how can that be more Antichristian than
> any other, seeing there is no certain government in the
> Word?[34]

Goodwin *had* caught Prynne and Coleman out, but not quite in
the way that he thought. Neither Prynne nor Coleman was a

doctrinaire Presbyterian; neither believed that Scripture prescribed one set of government above all others. But their readiness to see episcopacy as Antichristian had not derived from a commitment to Presbyterianism, although it might appear so in the euphoric climate of 1641–43. It derived, instead, from a millenarian reading of Scripture. Once indeed, Prynne, following Foxe, had seen Antichrist as Rome; then, expanding Foxe, he had expanded his concept of Antichrist to accommodate the phenomenon of Laudianism. By 1641, Prynne believed that Antichrist included Papists, Laudians *and indeed all bishops*. So too with Coleman: bishops had 'been burdensome in all ages' in England, and 'all Reformed Religions in the world have expelled them, as incompatible with Reformation'. The Covenant left no loophole for a 'regulated Episcopacy'. It looked to 'a new Government, and no Prelacy'.[35]

When Prynne and Coleman, by the time of the Erastian controversy, are expressing a sympathy with moderate Anglicanism, it is a retreat, not from Presbyterianism but from centrifugal millenarianism. To Hobbes and Selden the prattling about 'Antichrist' from either would have seemed grotesque. Hobbes had been reluctant even to call the Pope Antichrist: good grounds for calling Hobbes a Papist to some! And Selden said:

> They are both equally mad who say Bishops are soe *Iure Divino* that they must be continued and they who say that they are soe Antichristian that they must be put away. All is as the State likes.[36]

To the doctrinaire Presbyterian the moral laxity of the times had a less traumatic effect than it had upon men such as Prynne and Coleman. A party man, such as Gillespie, could take the moral breakdown in his stride. When Prynne asked Gillespie why he *should* value the disciplinary powers of excommunication when it was evident by 1645 – both in England and abroad – that the countries which lacked it had a more effective moral code than those which had it, Gillespie retorted that the raising of moral standards would be the natural consequence of a Scottish 'sin-searching, sin-discovering and sin-censuring discipline' in England. In the heady atmosphere of 1641 this evasion might have satisfied Prynne. In 1645 he wanted more solid reassurances. This does not mean that Prynne's judgement was superior to that of the Presbyterian ministers. Their belief, that moral laxity was the price of delay in setting up the discipline that they wanted, may have been correct. But the point was that their commitment to the party programme caused them to play down the importance of this moral laxity. Because Prynne was uncommitted, the ethical question stayed in the foreground. If the party programme was not fulfilling the ethical aim, Prynne was too uncompromising and obsessional to mask his impatience.

And patently the party programme was *not* fulfilling the ethical aim. Prynne recognised in 1645 – as did Coleman – that his faith in the London ministers had been misplaced. Not entirely: Prynne continued to admire them as individuals. They had advocated 'a thorough and compleat Reformation' in their sermons, and they had persistently warned their listeners that 'lesse will not be accepted of God or good men'. What had changed – and this is crucial – was not Prynne's admiration for the London ministers but his belief that *they were a representative body*.

Now – in 1645 – he saw that their zeal was atypical:

> That though there be sufficient choice of prudent, discreet, learned, conscientious, upright Ministers and Christians in and about London, fit to be united into Presbyteries, Classes, and trusted with Ecclesiasticall censures; yet in most places else throughout our three Kingdomes (except here and there a City or Country Town) there are very few, if any, such Ministers or Lay-Elders to be found for the present.[37]

It would be wrong to say that the Presbyterians had no answer to the breakdown of society, except the imposition of a full 'godly discipline'. That was the perfect solution. Meantime a start could be made by refusing to admit to the Sacraments the impure. And, in making this demand, the ministers revived all the suspicions that Erastus had voiced earlier: they resurrected Erastianism. Ministers were glad to stigmatise opposition to their demand as an 'Erastian' indifference to morality. But the opposition *was* Erastian in the true, not the pejorative, sense of the word: it was derived from Erastus, and shared with Erastus a great concern for morality. True Erastians such as Coleman and Prynne, favoured common admission to the Sacraments as a means of administering discipline, not the reverse. When Prynne wanted to see more members of Lincoln's Inn attending the Sacrament of the Lord's Supper, he cited orders made in the past to that effect by Benchers of Lincoln's Inn. His comment is significant:

> How well they deserve to feel the rod of the antient Discipline of the Society... which Godly Discipline I heartily wish may now be carefully revived.[38]

No wonder that Coleman became angry when Gillespie called him a 'Parliament Parasite'; as he pointed out, his way was 'as active and passive for the Church-refining and sinne-censuring government of Christ as any other'.[39] Indeed, he could point to the ministers' failure to effect moral reform hitherto and contrast this with the high ethical standards that had prevailed in England, even under 'a Prelaticall Tyranie'. It was facile to see the present malaise as the result of an *absence* of clerical discipline. This was to overlook the basic philosophical reason why no theocracy *could* implement a moral code:

> It is a Fallacy, taking that to be the Cause which is not: For look among whom have these irregularities most abounded here in London; some separated congregations are they that yielded us such a bad harvest; yet they had all Church Censures among them, and Excommunication it selfe.[40]

When the Presbyterian ministers took as the criterion of an effective discipline the purity of the ordinances, rather than the moral welfare of the people as a whole, they had undermined the ethical basis of their rule. As another Erastian, John Timson, put it:

> Did you intend the Reformation of the whole, or of a part only? If you be only for the reformation of a part, and your desire be to draw up some to purity of ordinance... what must become of all the rest?[41]

To say that the Erastians turned to a 'Godly Parliament' is

to get the emphasis wrong. It is to fall into the trap set by the Scottish ministers. The Erastians were very little concerned about the powers of Parliament: this was a concern fathered on them by their opponents. Like Erastus himself, they were more concerned with opposing the discipline than with exalting the magistrate. When the Commons allowed the principle of suspension – and the Erastians went on attacking the principle – opponents thought that they had caught them in an inconsistency.[42] Again and again, clericalists scold the Erastians for starting a controversy 'against the votes and judgments of a Parliament'.[43] But in truth this was no inconsistency, precisely because the Erastians were *not* 'Parliament Parasites'.

So the Erastian revival, far from being a reaction against the ideal of 'Godly Rule', is a continuation of it in a different form. England must be reformed: there is need for godly preachers: Antichrist will be overcome. This was Coleman's message in 1643, and it remained his message in 1645. Gillespie asked in ringing tones: 'What Apollo can reconcile Mr. Colemans Doctrine with the Covenant?'[44] But one does not need an Apollo; simply a recognition that the Covenant and Erastianism could be called into being by the same ethical impulse. Gillespie's colleagues gave this recognition, albeit grudgingly. Newcomen, in a sermon to the Commons in September 1644, pointed to the connection between the growth of dangerous ideas that 'there is no *Ius Divinum* upon the calling of the Ministry' with the failure to establish a moral code. As Newcomen said:

> We have Covenanted against Prophanenesse. But what hath been done against it? . . . for want of a strict course prescribed . . . Sabbaths and Fasts are as much contemned as ever.[45]

Similarly, Thomas Edwards noted the moral concern expressed by Coleman and Prynne:

> and this is a great Objection in the mindes and mouthes of many, especially those who are for the Erastian way.[46]

And Edward Terry saw that the moral breakdown threw into question the Presbyterian discipline that he still wished to see established in England:

But this I am sure of, that there is an intollerable, and un-answerable fault some where, when so much wickednesse goes unpunished, when so many errors, schisms, heresies . . . are suffered amongst us, though we have lifted up our hands unto the most high God in a solemne League and Covenant to the contrarie.[47]

Terry's diagnosis is very similar to Prynne's: both found 'intollerable' the dishonouring of the Covenant. But in one important respect they differ. Terry found the fault 'unanswerable'. As a committed Presbyterian he shrank from Prynne's Erastian answer: that 'reall speedy reformation in our Church' *could* not come from that 'strict discipline, which really reforms very few, or none'.[48]

A view of the Erastian revival that places it outside the 'Godly Rule' movement is wrong; they belong together. But this is not to say that, in a more indirect and subtle way, the Erastian revival did *not* harm the expectations of 'Godly Rule'.

This was how it came about. Bound up inseparably with the concept of 'Godly Rule' was confidence in the ability to read the Mind of God: to know the type of rule that would be pleasing to Him. This confidence was to be found especially in Calvinists. Not exclusively so. Sir Edward Coke's daughter was no Calvinist. Indeed, her favourite authors were Hooker, Andrewes and Jeremy Taylor. But she gives the classic expression of this brutal moralising when she seeks to dissuade Roger Williams from admiring Milton: 'You should have taken notice off God's judgment upon him who stroke him with blindness'.[49] But it is still more common to hear about 'God's judgment' from the committed Calvinist. Strictly speaking there is no reason why this should be so. It was, after all, a central tenet of Calvinism that God was Inscrutable.

But this was part of the paradox of Calvinism: the Elect *wills* the salvation which he cannot *earn*. Few books were as popular in the first half of the seventeenth century in England as Thomas Beard's *The Theatre of Gods Judgments*. This was the book in which Calvinists opened the secrets of history. Every seemingly accidental mishap, under Beard's steady scrutiny, was revealed as a Judgement of the Lord upon the transgressor. It was a book that comforted Oliver Cromwell; and the book, as much as any, that cost Prynne his ears.[50] Beard continued to be obligatory reading on the Sabbath in certain areas of Scotland late in the eighteenth century: the Scots relished, in Beard, such uplifting tales as that of the nobleman who used to hunt on the Lord's Day during sermons and, as a judgement, 'his wife gave birth to a child who had a head like a dog and howled like a hound'.[51] It was with the confidence of a Beard that the 'root and branch' ministers looked to the cleansing of England in 1641. What more natural than that the non-reformation of England should be seen as a mark of God's Wrath? In vain for the Scot, Rutherford, to argue that once a true Presbyterian discipline was set up in England, corresponding to the ideals of Thomas Cartwright, the moral reformation *would* take place.[52] His colleague, Terry, had already conceded that the failure to effect that moral reformation had damaged the Presbyterian cause. The Presbyterians could not have it both ways. If Coleman's death was a Judgement of God, so too was the *indestructibility of his ideas*.

In showing that the moral breakdown was a consequence of clericalism, the Erastians were still operating within the confines of Beard's own didactic philosophy. But Coleman went further. In one sermon to the Commons in 1644, he did not merely say that the Presbyterian ministers were wrong to see recent actions as a sign of God's approval of their cause. He asked: how far can *anyone* be sure that he has God's approval? And, in asking that question, he moved away from the premises of 'Godly Rule' and closer to the premise of Hobbes. His colleague, Newcomen, had interpreted the breakdown of order as a Judgement of God. This was not how Coleman saw it:

> We have prayed to our God, his answer is rough, by terrible things: yet in this answer, is himselfe most righteous, and in the issue to us, a saving God.

For we delude ourselves when we claim to read God's Mind:

> That which may be knowne of God (for something may,

though little) that little, then, that shamefull little (as the word
seemes to import), in respect of our apprehending it, is transmitted to our understandings in Scripture by such termes,
which we peculiarly call Attributes . . . .[53]

This is pure Hobbes. Hobbes had argued that we can only
speak of God in a series of negatives such as 'infinite', 'immut-
able', 'incomprehensible', or in terms signifying His remote-
ness from our mortal state, such as 'omnipotent', 'most high' and
the like. These are 'pseudo-statements', telling us nothing of
the object worshipped, but something of the attitude of the
worshipper:

> . . . for in the Attributes which we give to God we are not
> to consider the signification of Philosophical Truth, but the
> signification of Pious Intention, to do him the greatest Honour
> we are able.

And like Hobbes, Coleman believed that the one thing that we
knew of God was His Power. As Coleman argued:

> So from the Creation, an act of power, we call God Power-
> full; from that admirable order, wherein all things were dis-
> posed, we call him Wise . . . so the Saints in their prayers,
> according to the subject of their Petitions, entitle him Great,
> Most High, Preserver of men, Hearer of Prayers and like.

And of the Psalm – 'by terrible things in righteousness wilt
thou answer us, O God of our Salvation' – Coleman has this
to say: that 'terrible things' mean 'such actings of thy Power
and Providence, as may strike terrour into men, and cause
them to tremble, reverencing thy presence above all Gods'. For
Coleman believed, as much as Hobbes did, that fear cements
the commonweath; and that prayer is the symptom of fear:

> They pray indeed but it is when they are ready to drop into
> Hell, when they are on their beds of sicknesse and death, lest
> they should be damned.[55]

The full significance of this sermon can only be understood
if it is compared with one that Coleman delivered only a year
before, *The Christians Course and Complaint*. Coleman had then
confidently told the Commons that God *did* speak to Man. He

showed three ways in which Man could read God's Mind. First, by prayer: he expected 'Gods praying suppliants' to meet with the success of a Hannah when she prayed for a child:

> such an internall answer revealed to her soule, which did so assure her of successe, that rising from prayer, she looked no more sad.

Second, by a Beard-like vigilance to read, in the seeming accident, 'Gods voyce for their own good'. Third, by sensitivity to what Coleman called 'ensuing occurrents'. These were distinguished from accidents by being events which yielded significance, not through being studied *in isolation* but through being studied *in the context of* other events. By this inspired form of 'pigeon-holing' Man came to God. Coleman demonstrated what this meant in 1643:

> Such as these, Scotland satisfied in their pursuit: This Parliament beyond expectation gathered; beyond example continued; so many hellish designes discovered; and the mischief of them prevented; yea, turned upon them, in whom they first bred: such a praying spirit in all hearts, so many dayes of prayer, publike, private: such respect to the best both men and Ministers; such Covenants, Protestations, Oathes; this present now in agitation for the union of the Kingdomes; such laying to heart our Cause in France, Low Countries and other Reformed Churches; such brotherly, and tender affections, and expressions in Scotland; and (which is not the least) the Assembly called, and sitting, Reformation going on, the Citie of God erecting, even in a troublesome time, as Daniel foretold it should.

We know God, in short, by making intelligent lists. Coleman, in the 1643 sermon, captures the authentic flavour of the 'root and branch' times right down to the optimistic chiliasm that foresaw a New Jerusalem arising from the rubble. And the summation of Coleman's list, the most hopeful of all the 'ensuing occurrents', was: the Assembly of Divines, the continuing Reformation, the coming Apocalypse. The contrast between the euphoria of 1643 and the wry defeatism of 1644 is poignant and moving. It telescopes in one year the process by which many Calvinists lost their faith in a 'Godly Rule'.

By 1644 Coleman was sounding like Hobbes. The importance of his sermon then as an anticipation of some of the principles of Hobbes's *Leviathan* has never been sufficiently stressed. This, of course, in no way lessens Hobbes's influence or significance. But it points to something else: to our tendency too often to read secularisation simply in terms of the cynical thrusts of inveterate anti-clericalists. The fact that, in one sermon, Coleman sounded like Hobbes is less important than our realisation of the gap that still separated the Erastian from the 'Parliament-Parasite'. Coleman and his fellow-Erastians were moved, not by cynicism, but by passion. Nevertheless, they were moved in the direction of Hobbes.

The retreat from 'Godly Rule' was led by its former partisans. Originally they had been inflamed by a vision from Scripture of the imminent downfall of Antichrist. So long as men believed in prince or bishop or minister as the instrument of destruction the more anarchical implications of the vision were held in check. When that check disappeared men were left with their own intimations. But since one man's intimations were another man's delusions, the way was open for endless quarrels: a Hobbesian state of nature. Cromwell was to perceive this in the course of the Putney Debates. The way out of the impasse would have been for him to impose his own vision on that of his colleagues. We shall see in the next chapter why Cromwell shrank from this solution and settled for something seemingly less: a 'Godless Rule'.

The idea of a 'Godly Rule' had only ever been tenable on the assumption that God's Will was intelligible. The concept was to become debased in Cromwell's eyes when Levellers such as Wildman and Rainborough invoked it, as it had already become in Coleman's eyes when Presbyterian Scots such as Gillespie and Baillie invoked it. But the alternative was not to disown Calvinism; rather, it was to reinterpret Calvinism more rigorously. For, although we have seen that the concept is Calvinist, it is also in another sense truly non-Calvinist. For, although the identification of self with the workings of God's Purpose is a characteristic of the Calvinist Elect, it runs counter to another

Calvinist principle: that we do not know who the Elect are; God is Inscrutable. There is in the Calvinist mind a constant tension between the two impulses. It is a fair criticism of Max Weber's identification of the Calvinist ethic and capitalism that he puts disproportionate weight on the tendency among Calvinists to see worldly prosperity as a reliable indication of God's favour.[56] He fails to emphasise the extent to which Calvinists placed equal weight on the *inscrutability* of God: the wicked prospered; the virtuous were cast down. And Sibbes warned that worldly success was 'digging a pit for the wicked'.[57] It is true that Cromwell identified those with 'the root of the matter in them' as those who fought bravely on his side. But that was a war-time criterion; in peace, there was no simple index of godliness.[58]

The Calvinists were in a peculiarly strong position to repudiate those who identified their will with God's; that is, if they did not worry too much about personal consistency. No man in the thirties had been more familiar with God's Designs than William Prynne. With enviable confidence (quoting frequently from Beard) he ransacked history for God's Judgements on those who had performed stage plays.

This did not prevent him later from feeling outraged when some opponents, with Prynne-like ingenuity, showed how people who seized the estates of clergymen invariably met with sticky ends. It was from a secure Calvinist base that Prynne launched his attack:

> these Authors upon groundlesse conjectures over-boldly assert, *as if they were privy to God's secrets,* whose judgments are unsearchable and his wayes past finding out.[59]

And it is important to realise that Prynne attacked the claim of Presbyterian and Independent ministers to suspend the unworthy from the Sacraments on the grounds that it was inconsistent with the Calvinist concept of Grace. Ministers were presumptuous in trying to read God's Mind. They had forgotten that indeed 'God can sodainly change notorious sinners hearts, lives, and bring them to repentance in a moment, before

Ministers can take reall notice of it'.[60] A critic later would make
the point that Prynne himself had not observed these maxims
so closely when he had been waging his crusade against scandalous behaviour, in pamphlets, such as *Histriomastix*, against
stage plays. He reminded Prynne that, in that pamphlet of
1633, he had referred to an incident where two actors had
been converted when blasphemously joking about taking the
Sacraments. He asked, if Prynne had been a minister, whether
he would have admitted to the Lord's Table persons 'that had
lately committed but a Mimical Rape, or acted the Divel upon
a Stage'? The writer put the alternative to Prynne:

> If nay; then Mr. Prynne is ours. If yea; What meant Mr.
> Prynne to make (or my self and others to buy at so dear a
> rate) that seven stringed whip (a book of great reading, and
> then of as great zeal) called *Histriomastix*.[61]

The presentation of the alternatives in this form was plausible,
but unjust to Prynne. The basic premise was false. Prynne's
Histriomastix had been, it is true, a blueprint for ethical
reform; but for ethical reform which would come through the
agency of the Christian Emperor, not through more stringent
and ambitious disciplinary claims by the clergy.

It was understandable that the critics of Prynne's position
in the 1640s should contrast his position then with his days 'of
great zeal' in the 1630s. One of the London 'root and branch'
ministers also accused Prynne in 1645 of having become lukewarm, of having rejected zeal and Thomas Brightman:

> Mr. Brightman (whose interpretation of Revel. 3 concerning
> Sardis and Laodicea, have been to admiration and neare to
> Propheticall) makes England, as you know, the Anti-type of
> the latter: surely whoever thinks he is at all in the right
> therein, and withall have seene that lukewarme Angell so
> strangely spawned out ... ought to take speciall heed, that
> they themselves degenerate not into like lukewarmnesse.[62]

Prynne was no more lukewarm about ethical reforms in the
1640s than Coleman was. If he argued against debarring
offenders from the Sacraments it was not (as his critic tried to
make out) because he no longer cared, as he once had done,

about 'mimical rapes' or acting 'the Devil upon a stage'. It was rather because he felt (as Erastus had felt against Wither in Heidelberg) that the suspending clergymen had despaired too soon of reforming the ungodly. The two actors had approached the Sacraments in a mocking spirit; they had been conquered by God's Power.

So too Hobbes was impeccably Calvinist when he scolded Wallis in 1662 for 'this bold Undertaking of yours, to consider and decypher Gods nature to us', or when he scorned the Schoolmen for 'their bold opinions concerning the incomprehensible nature of God'. And Hobbes's favourite book of Scripture was the Book of Job: in the sufferings of Job, the capricious – and unaccountable – power of God was most triumphantly displayed. Cudworth was perspicacious enough to see Calvin in Hobbes, although he distinguished Hobbes's 'Divine Fatalism Natural' from Calvin's 'Divine Fatalism Arbitrary'.[63] The omnipotent, uncensurable sovereign to whom Hobbes surrendered power had a face like Calvin's God.

Coleman and his fellow-Erastians did not fight the clerics in order to set up a 'Godly Parliament'. Like Erastus himself, they claimed little more than that the magistrate could achieve more successfully the ethical reform which the clergy were professedly aiming to carry out. Their emphasis is quite different from Hobbes's. They thought that religion was too important to be entrusted to clergymen; he thought that religion was so unimportant – albeit dangerous – that it should be left to the civil magistrate. But they converged in recognising the hollowness of the theocrats' claim to represent God's Will. While Coleman and his fellow-Erastians were merely emphasising the failure of the Westminster Assembly and the dishonouring of the Covenant as signs of God's Displeasure, they were still talking the language of 'Godly Rule'. When they took the further step of generalising from this experience – of emphasising the inadequacy of *any* attempt to read God's Mind – they were moving beyond 'Godly Rule' and towards Hobbes.

God is Omnipotent: this Calvinist truism was the basis of 'Godly Rule'. But in repudiating 'Godly Rule', there was no need for Calvinists to repudiate the truism. All they needed to do was to give the truism a different emphasis. For it is a moot point whether the Omnipotence of God is more evident in His Caprice than in His Design. John Hampden killed 'in the same place in which he had first executed the ordinance of the militia'; the Sabbath-breaking huntsman who begat a hound-child; Thomas Coleman struck down with a mortal illness for defying the Westminster Assembly; incest and adultery abounding because the Westminster Assembly had failed to put its house in order: all these are striking manifestations of God's Omnipotence. But it is arguable that the boils that plagued the virtuous Job are as much a manifestation of God's Power as the Cavalier corpses on Marston Moor. The Inscrutability of God is at least as legitimate an inference from the doctrine of Predestination as the Design of God; but it subverts the very idea of a 'Godly Rule'.

For 'Godly Rule' presupposes an ability to read God's Mind. This can be achieved by studying Scripture (above all, the Book of Revelation); by prayer; by studying history (with the help of inspired interpreters such as Thomas Beard and William Prynne). Men who carry out any of these activities *know*, for example, that gambling is displeasing to God; that remedial action must be taken; that if remedial action is not taken, God's Retribution will be terrible. Contrast their position with that of a Thomas Browne. Browne was a Calvinist who accepted wholeheartedly the dogma of Predestination. But he took the terror from it – of a God who knowingly consigns most of mankind to eternal damnation before they are born – by emphasising, with Hobbes, the presumption of seeking to measure God by the yard-sticks and time-scales of Man. God is not bound by time: 'What to us is to come, to his eternity is present.' Therefore it follows that predestination is 'in respect to God' not a determination of 'our estates to come, but a definitive blast of his will already fulfilled, and at the instant that he first decreed it'. This is impeccable Calvinist theology; one also feels that it is too clever by half. In the controversy over Free Will, both sides were fighting over vital issues, which Browne artfully sidesteps. God *can* be all-powerful; Man *can* be free. This does not so much explain the problem as explain it away. But its consequences are important for Browne. No longer can we be sure that a pastime such as gambling *is* displeasing to God. It may be; it may not be. God is indecipherable. And so the prudent Browne concludes that 'tis not a ridiculous devotion to say a prayer before a game at tables'. Praying, for Browne, is – as it was for Hobbes and Coleman – the propitiation of a wayward Deity; not – as it was to be for the rival cliques among the Army officers at Putney – an exercise at identifying one's will with God's.[64]

Most important, Browne has no time for the millenarian speculations of a Foxe or Brightman:

> Now to determine the day and year of this inevitable time, is not only convincible and statute-madness, but also manifest impiety.

A sceptic could see the madness; it took a Calvinist to see the impiety. Browne was as scornful as Hobbes ever was of the idea of Antichrist. He said that 'the common sign drawn from the revelation of Antichrist, is as obscure as any'. He even called Antichrist 'the Philosopher's stone in Divinity'. The Book of Job had conquered the Book of Revelation.[65]

1. Thomas Brightman, *A Revelation of the Revelation . . .* (Amsterdam, 1615) p. 559, warns against such speculations; although Hanserd Knollys, *A Glimpse of Sions Glory* (London, 1641) p. 32, thanked Brightman for just such an insight.

2. E. Tuveson, *Millennium and Utopia*, p. 87.

3. G. R. Abernathy, Jun., *The English Presbyterians and the Stuart Restoration: 1648–1663* (Philadelphia, American Philosophical Society, 1965).

4. *The Moderate Intelligencer*, No. 28 (4–11 September 1445).

5. Herbert Palmer, *The Glasse of Gods Providence* (London, 1644) p. 35.

6. Thomas Wilson, *Davids Zeale for Zion . . .*, p. 14.

7. Samuel Fairclough, *The Troublers Troubled . . .* (London,

1641) pp. 37–8; Thomas Case, *The Second Sermon*..., pp. 29–32, 56; Nathaniel Holmes, *The New World*... (London, 1641) p. 29; Joseph Symonds, *A Sermon*... (London, 1641) no pagination.

8. George Morley, *A Sermon*... (London, 1641) p. 14.

9. Thomas Hill, *The Sermon for England's Selfe-Reflection* ... (London, 1644) p. 34.

10. Robert Baillie, *Letters and Journals*..., II 199.

11. Valerie Pearl, 'Oliver St John and the "middle group" in the Long Parliament, August 1643–May 1644,' *English Historical Review* LXXXI, 320 (July 1966) pp. 496–500 especially.

12. John Selden, *Table Talk*, ed. F. Pollock (London, Quaritch, 1927) p. 125 Cf. E. Tuveson, *Millennium and Utopia*, p. 79: 'the great reform wave which had given rise to the Westminster Assembly'.

13. Baillie, *Letters and Journals*, II 315.

14. Cornelius Burges, *The First Sermon*..., p. 35.

15. Baillie, *Letters and Journals*, I 302–3; cf. the trenchant criticism of Burges's 'captiousness' in refusing initially to take the Covenant in John Lightfoot, *Works*, XIII 11. Lightfoot, like Coleman, was an Erastian who cared deeply about the Covenant – and its non-fulfilment later.

16. Jeremiah Burroughs, *Sions Joy* (London, 1641) p. 54.

17. (Doctor Williams's Library) Baxter MSS. 59.3, f. 115, f. 251.

18. *The Scottish Dove*, No. 56 and No. 58; Baillie, *Letters and Journals*, II 122, 111, 313, 260. The converse to this is that a New England divine such as Cotton Mather could lament that not all English Presbyterians were like Stephen Marshall: *The Puritans*... ed. P. Miller and T. Johnson, I 178.

19. J. N. Figgis, 'Erastus and Erastianism', *Journal of Theological Studies*, II (1900) 73, 71, 85, 88, 65, 81.

20. George Gillespie, *Aarons Rod Blossoming*...; Samuel Rutherford, *The Divine Right of Church-Government and Excommunication*... (London, 1646).

21. George Gillespie, *Nihil Respondis* ... (London, 1645) p. 31; *Aarons Rod Blossoming*..., p. 168.

22. George Gillespie, *A Sermon*... (London, 1645) p. 33. For Coleman's activities against clericalism in the Westminster Assembly, see *Minutes of the Sessions of the Westminster Assembly of Divines*, ed. A. Mitchell and J. Struthers (Edinburgh, 1874) pp. 33, 117, 118, 119, 193, 194.

23. Baillie, *Letters and Journals*, II 360.

24. Gillespie, *Aarons Rod Blossoming*..., p. 168; Baillie, *Letters and Journals*, II 364.

25. Robert Bacon, *The Spirit of Prelacie Yet Working* (London, 1646) dedicatory epistle; Christopher Cartwright, *The Magistrates Authority in Matters of Religion*... (London, 1647) dedicatory epistle.

26. Francis Woodcock, *Lex Talionis*... (London, 1645) dedicatory epistle.

27. Thomas Case, *The Quarrell of the Covenant*... (London, 1643) p. 53; Thomas Edwards, *Gangraena* ..., dedicatory epistle; Daniel Featley, *The League Illegal* (London, 1643) p. 17.

28. Thomas Fuller, *The Church History of Britain*, ed. J. Brewer (Oxford, J. H. & J. Parker, 1845) VI 286.

29. (Doctor Williams's Library) Baxter MSS. 59.6, f. 192v.

30. Ibid. 59.3, f. 115.

31. Thomas Coleman, *The Christians Course and Complaint* ... (London, 1643) dedicatory epistle.

32. Selden, *Table Talk* ..., p. 107; Hobbes, *English Works* ..., VI 242.

33. Coleman, *The Christians Course*, pp. 24, 68.

34. John Goodwin, *Certaine Briefe Observations*... (London, 1645) p. 3.

35. Coleman, *The Hearts Ingagement*... (London, 1643) pp. 23, 36–8. So that Baxter was wrong to try to defend Coleman's consistency on the grounds that the Covenant, while rooting out *iure divino* episcopacy, said nothing about 'excluding simple episcopacy': (Doctor Williams's Library) Baxter MSS. 59.3, f. 116.

36. Selden, *Table Talk*, p. 20.

37. William Prynne, *A Vindication of Four Serious Questions*... (London, 1645) p. 89, dedicatory epistle. In the draft Declaration that the Commons drew up in late 1645 on suspension from the Sacrament, this very point was made: 'Neither are we only ... to look upon the ministers of the City of London ... but throughout the whole Kingdom also': Historical Manuscripts Commission, *13th Report*, I 297.

38. Prynne, *An Appendix to a Seasonable Vindication of Free-Admission*... (London, 1657) pp. 2, 9.

39. Thomas Coleman, *Maledicis* ..., p. 18.

40. Coleman, *A Brotherly Examination Re-Examined*..., pp. 2, 3, 10.

41. John Timson, *The Bar to Free Admission to the Lords Supper Removed* (London, 1654) p. 85.

42. The First Parliamentary Ordinance for Scandal of 20 October 1645 had conceded the principle of suspension, but had rejected the ministers' claim to exercise this disciplinary power by *iure divino* authority: (British Museum) Thomason Tracts E. 305/13: *Ordinance of Lords and Commons ... 20 October 1645* ..., pp. 7–9. The Erastian Prynne had six days earlier been appointed one of the Triers of the elders for the classis at the Inns of Court. Prynne would be cleared of inconsistency only if he limited his attack on suspension to the *iure divino* claim, and not to the principle itself. He professed to do this in a pamphlet of 1646. He disclaimed any intention of arguing against suspension 'by virtue of a meere Parliamentary sanction' and promised that the pamphlet would refer only 'to that pretended divine Authority, will and appointment of Jesus Christ, by which our Divines now claime it'. This distinction is swiftly blurred in the rest of the pamphlet. See: William Prynne, *Suspention Suspended ...* (London, 1646). And his critics were not slow to point this out: (Anon.), *A Vindication of Two Serious Questions ...* (London, 1646) pp. 24, 42, 55; Gillespie, *Aarons Rod Blossoming ...*, p. 340.

43. Roger Drake, *The Bar Against Free Admission to the Lords Supper Fixed ...* (London, 1655) p. 275.

44. Gillespie, *Nihil Respondis ...*, p. 30.

45. Matthew Newcomen, *A Sermon ...* (London, 1644) pp. 36, 39.

46. Thomas Edwards, *Gangraena ...*, p. 114.

47. Edward Terry, *Lawlesse Liberty ...* (London, 1646) p. 7.

48. Prynne, *A Vindication of Foure Serious Questions ...*, p. 57.

49. Miller and Johnson (eds.), *The Puritans,* II 482.

50. Thomas Beard, *The Theatre of Gods Judgments* (London, 1631): this was the third edition of this classic, quoted extensively by Prynne in his *Histriomastix,* the book which was the cause of Prynne's first trial in 1634. For Beard's influence on Cromwell, see Maurice Ashley, *The Greatness of Oliver Cromwell* (London, Hodder, 1958) p. 43.

51. H. G. Graham, *The Social Life of Scotland in the Eighteenth Century* (London, Black, 1950) p. 318.

52. Rutherford, *The Divine Right of Church-Government ...* (n.d.) pp. 640–1.

53. Thomas Coleman, *Gods Unusuall Answer ...* (London, 1644) p. 3.

54. Thomas Hobbes, *Leviathan ...* (Everyman's Library) p. 195.

55. Coleman, *Gods Unusuall Answer,* pp. 2, 12.

56. Max Weber, *The Protestant Ethic and the Spirit of Capitalism* (London, Unwin University Books, 1965) p. 112.

57. C. H. and K. George, *The Protestant Mind of the English Reformation, 1570–1640,* pp. 161–2.

58. Christopher Hill, *Oliver Cromwell, 1658–1958* (Historical Association Pamphlet, No. 38) p. 10.

59. William Prynne, *A Postscript Concerning Sacrilege . . .,* (London, 1658) p. 134. My italics.

60. Prynne, *Four Serious Questions . . .* (London, 1644), no pagination.

61. S.S., *Holy Things for Holy Men . . .* (London, 1658) p. 16.

62. Herbert Palmer, *A Full Answer to a Printed Paper . . .,* (London, 1645) p. 25. He chides Prynne (pp. 4–5), 'Do not your self know, even by experience, that no man can shew zeal against scandalous sinnes, but by some, and even to many, he will seem to runne into Extremes'.

63. Samuel Mintz, *The Hunting of Leviathan* (Cambridge University Press, 1962) p. 127.

64. A. S. P. Woodhouse, ed., *Puritanism and Liberty,* pp. 21–38.

65. Thomas Browne, *Religio Medici* (Everyman's Library) pp. 32, 34, 51, 52.

6 Godless Rule

> Under the sad sufferings of the people of God our souls
> mourned, and understanding by the manifold gracious
> promises in the word of God, that a time of deliverance
> was to be expected to the Church of Christ, and destruc-
> tion and ruin to Babylon, our hearts, together with all
> the true godly in England were exceedingly stirred up
> to pray to the Lord, even day and night, that he would
> arise to destroy Antichrist, and to save his people ... we
> found our hearts extraordinarily stirred up by the Lord,
> to assist the Parliament against the King, being abso-
> lutely satisfied in our judgments and consciences that we
> were called forth by the Lord to be instrumental to
> bring about that which was our continual prayer to God,
> viz., the destruction of Antichrist, and the deliverance
> of his Church and people ... we were then powerfully
> convinced that the Lord's purpose was to deal with the
> late king as a man of blood. And being persuaded in our
> consciences that he and his monarchy was one of the ten
> horns of the Beast (spoken of, Rev. 17 : 12–15) and
> being witnesses to so much of the innocent blood of the
> Saints that he had shed in supporting the Beast, and con-
> sidering the loud cries of the souls of the Saints under
> the altar, we were extraordinarily carried forth to desire
> justice upon the King, that man of blood.[1]

These extracts from the Declaration of the English Army in
Scotland, on 1 August 1650, make fascinating reading. They
impose coherence upon the events of the previous decade. The
Book of Revelation [the argument runs] comforted the godly in
the time of Laud's persecutions, inspired them to take up arms for
Parliament at the beginning of the Civil War and steeled them to
execute their king at the end of the Civil War. All this was true.

But it was not the whole truth. As we have seen already, millenarianism was not the property of one extremist wing of the Army. It had coloured the thinking of Anglicans under the spell of Foxe, and of 'root and branch' ministers under the spell of Brightman. It had even – more surprisingly – influenced those who led the Erastian challenge towards the end of the Civil War. The drafters of the Declaration had no qualms, however, about appropriating the Apocalypse to themselves. At the time when they wrote, might seemed to be on their side: their commentary on the past was intended to be a preamble to the decisive acts of the future. 'The Lord has brought us hither by his providence,' they said, with a certain complacency, 'and upon him we shall with confidence depend till we see a glorious issue.'[2]

Their confidence depended upon God, it is true, but also upon the leadership of Oliver Cromwell. Here was the Godly Ruler to fulfil the prophecies of Revelation: who better to execute the Judgements of God than the devout reader of the *Theatre of Gods Judgments*?

The Commonwealth, however, was to see, not the fulfilment of 'Godly Rule', but its denial. This does not mean that Cromwell was not stirred by similar aspirations. His hunger for a 'Godly Rule' was never more manifest than in his letter to Colonel Walton after the victory at Marston Moor:

> It had all the evidences of an absolute victory obtained by the Lord's Blessing upon the Godly Party principally. We never charged but we routed the enemy ... God made them as stubble to our swords. ... There is your precious child full of glory, never to know sin or sorrow any more. He was a gallant young man, exceedingly gracious. God give you His comfort. Before his death he was so full of comfort that to Frank Russell and myself he could not express it, 'It was so great above his pain.' This he said to us. Indeed it was admirable. A little after, he said, One thing lay upon his spirit. I asked him, What that was? He told me it was, 'That God had not suffered him to be any more the executioner of His enemies'.[3]

Michael Walzer has rightly seen Cromwell's New Model Army as an embodiment of the attempt to set up a visible Kingdom of

Christ with 'its rigid camp discipline, its elaborate rules against every imaginable sin from looting and rapine to blasphemy and card-playing'.[4] If Cromwell had honoured the memory of Colonel Walton's son the Commonwealth should have become quite simply the New Model Army writ large. But, as Walzer himself admits, 'the rule of the Saints was brief, the new forms of repression were never enforced through the decisive activity of a state police'.[5] If they had been, the mind boggles at the thought of Hobbes becoming a citizen of Cromwell's Commonwealth. But Hobbes could make his peace with Cromwell precisely because he was not called on for membership of an army of Saints. The turning-point for Cromwell was Putney. In battle Cromwell had identified the Saints: those who had fought, and died, alongside him against Antichrist were those with the 'root of the matter' in them. The identification became fuzzy at Putney: those whom he had thought to be saints were denouncing property! Worse, they were as confident as he that they were interpreting God's Will correctly. No sharper lesson on the Inscrutability of God could have been provided. Cromwell believed that God had singled him out 'to wait for some extraordinary dispensations'. His opponents believed the same. Cromwell called their intimations 'imaginary apprehensions' of 'divine impressions and divine discoveries'. But why were *their* intimations imaginary; *his* not? An embarrassed Cromwell could only claim that, when two parties asserted with equal sincerity that they were interpreting God's Will, the only safe rule was: 'Let the rest judge.'[6] But who were 'the rest'? It was a feeble evasion, but one could see why Cromwell made it. He was on firmer ground later when he argued in 1647, against the Agitators, the folly of fixing on Utopian *ends* and instead *urged* concentration on the *means*:

> There will be very great mountains in the way of this, if this were the thing in present consideration; and therefore we ought to consider the consequences, and God hath given us our reason that we may do this. *It is not enough to propose things that are good in the end*, but suppose this model were an excellent model, and fit for England and the kingdom to receive, it is our duty as Christians and men to *consider consequences, and to consider the way.*[7]

By directing men to the study of *means* rather than of *ends* Cromwell was, even in the Civil War, anticipating the changed concept of rule that was to mark his Protectorate. He would have his euphoric lapses, as when he hailed the Barebones Parliament with the words: 'You manifest this, as far as poor creatures can, to be the day of the power of Christ.' He would continue to identify Antichrist with the Papal enemy abroad, as in his speech to the Commons in 1656:

> Therefore I say that your danger is from the Common Enemy abroad; who is the head of the Papal Interest, the head of the Antichristian Interest – who is so described in Scripture, so forspoken of, and so fully, under that characteral name of Antichrist given him by the Apostle in the Epistle to the Thessalonians and likewise so expressed in the Revelations; which are sure and plain things! Except you will deny the truth of the Scriptures, you must needs see that that State is so described in Scripture to be Papal and Antichristian. I say, with this Enemy, and from this Account, you have the quarrel – with the Spaniard.[8]

The Revelations may be 'sure and plain things', but Cromwell cannot identify his *domestic* opponents with Antichrist with the same assurance that he identifies his *foreign* opponents. Indeed, he warns his son about the Anabaptists' presumptuousness in labelling those who disagree with them as Antichristian. He rebukes the Scottish General Assembly about the perils of 'spiritual drunkenness'. He boasts in 1655 that his greatest achievement has been that he has 'not been unhappy in hindering any one Religion to impose upon another'.[9] All this seems tame stuff after Marston Moor – does this merely represent the compromises of an ageing radical?

It certainly represents a *change* from Marston Moor:

> To dream of setting up an outward, glorious visible Kingdom of Christ, which hee might bear rule in ... be it in Germany or England, is but an unguarded presumption.

The words are not Cromwell's, but they could have been. They were those of his chaplain, John Owen, in 1652. They are the *nunc dimittis* of 'Godly Rule'. They are quoted by Michael Walzer to a different purpose. He sees them as distinguishing the Puritan revolutionary from the mere chiliast. He claims that Owen was translating 'the mystical Apocalypse into practical political terms'.[10] But this was dilution, not translation; a retreat from the Millennium, not an adaptation of it.[11] During the Civil War there had not been the same dichotomy between chiliasm and practical politics. This was the time when the New Model Army *was* creating a 'Godly Rule'. This was the time when Stephen Marshall denied that there was anything esoteric about apocalyptic interpretation (though characteristically overplaying his hand with the claim that '*the whole Army* of Protestant Interpreters' agreed on its scope and meaning[12]). This was the time when chiliasm *was* practical politics. But by 1652 this was palpable nonsense, when so many exotically radical sects were developing their own interpretations of the Apocalypse. It was then that a Puritan had to *separate* chiliasm from practical politics.

But while it is wrong to pretend that this did not involve Cromwell in a change from the days of Marston Moor, it would be equally wrong to represent the change as an acceptance of compromise. Indeed, it could be argued that the change represented a *refusal* to compromise. Roger Williams offers an instructive parallel here. Rather than settle for 'a rough approximation to the kingdom of God on earth',[13] Williams and Cromwell demanded the real thing or nothing at all. There was nothing half-hearted about the measures that either took to attain the real thing, although Williams went further in his quest than even Cromwell did. Williams proved that no church could attain purity in this world by a process of trial and error. He withdrew from the Church of England when it failed to measure up to his standards; then he withdrew from the churches of Massachusetts when they disappointed him; he ended up by withdrawing from everyone except his wife. Williams almost parodies the process by which men searched for a 'Godly Rule'. But what is fascinating in Williams's evolution is that it does not stop there. He learned, from his own experience, the futility of a search to set up an 'outward, glorious visible Kingdom of Christ', as much as Cromwell's chaplain had done. Then – and then only – Williams came to reject the idea of a coerced virtue. The kings of Israel, after all, were not examples of piety for Christian Emperors; their executions of heretics and of witches, after all, were not models for the modern magistrate to copy. Williams now saw that the magistrate must try to do no more than 'keep the peace', or, as Cromwell was to put it, be 'a good Constable set to keep the peace of the Parish'.[14] There had been a moment in time – for Williams with the Salem Church, for Cromwell with the New Model Army – when both felt the imminence of a 'Godly Rule' on earth. It was easy then – although, from a strict Calvinist point of view, heterodox – to identify the Elect, those with the 'root of the matter' in them, with respectively the saints of Salem and the Ironsides. How chastening then for Williams to see the visible saints refusing to renounce the other churches of Massachusetts, for Cromwell to see his comrades in arms refusing to recognise the rights of property at Putney. To their credit, both Williams and Cromwell did not turn, in disillusionment, to some shabby compromise. They would have no truck with some half-hearted attempt at a 'Godly Rule'. Instead they rejected the whole concept. The individual must now find his own salvation within the context of a rule that did not press too heavily upon his conscience. This was, we shall see, the quality that an opponent like Richard Baxter was to honour in Cromwell. And when Cromwell could look back on his rule and say that he had 'not been unhappy in hindering any one Religion to impose upon another' this was no apology for non-achievement. On the contrary, he called it 'the blessedest thing which hath been since the adventuring upon this Government'.[15] Only an idealist would have contented himself with the aim of becoming a good Constable.

This was a striking change of aspiration: the Godly Prince had become the good Constable. The fact that James I had not been a particularly inspiring Godly Prince; the fact that, in foreign affairs at least, Cromwell was to continue to use apocalyptic language – none of this should obscure the importance of this change of aspiration. England may never have had an Emperor Contantine; now she would never even *try* to have one. Yet this did not mean a slackening of interest in moral *behaviour*. Rather the reverse: antinomianism was associated with the 'lunatic fringe' sects of the Commonwealth, such as the Ranters, who continued to believe in the Apocalypse. No wonder Richard Baxter, abhorring Ranter excesses, would now abhor the millenarian dreams that had once stirred his imagination; and would try to conceal the fact that they ever *had* stirred his imagination. Contrariwise, he would be unable to withhold respect from a Protector who showed a real concern to redress moral excesses. For, as early as 1647, Cromwell had tacitly renounced the idea of a 'Godly Ruler', when he emphasised the importance of *means* rather than *ends*. So the real danger when he assumed full powers of leadership in the Commonwealth was not that he would impose a doctrinaire vision upon his subjects but that a more subtle temptation might present itself to him. If he believed that truth would not come from direction from the centre but from the action of individual congregations, might he not abandon the attempt to ensure minimum standards of order and decency? This Cromwell did not do; although he had friends to counsel him along these lines. Cromwell thought that a Christian government had a duty to provide sound ministers in *all* parishes. In 1654 Cromwell set up a central committee of 'Triers' by ordinance. Its task was to investigate the background and qualifications of candidates for collation to benefices or appointment to lectureships. This committee – and its successors – are to be regarded as Cromwell's efforts to secure that minimum standard of order and decency. The Triers wrung from Richard Baxter – no friend of Cromwell – grudging admiration: 'to give them their due, they did abundance of good to the Church. They saved many a congregation from ignorant, ungodly, drunken teachers.'[16] They did, in other words, more for public morality than the Church of England of Baxter's childhood had done, or for that matter the Westminster Assembly of Divines had done, despite all the propaganda of the London 'root and branch' ministers.

After the rule of Cromwell, nothing could be the same again. James I had seen himself – his subjects, reared on Foxe, had seen him – as the Christian Prince. This role Charles I had diffidently renounced for himself, *but not for his Church*. Nor had his Church – under a leader with Laud's vision – felt any diffidence about taking over that role. The Civil War left a vacuum at the centre: one that the Presbyterians had wished to fill with their discipline, and one that their Erastian opponents had wished to fill with Parliamentary action. Now for the first time – under Cromwell – there was a *deliberate* vacuum at the centre. Cromwell did not use this authority to impose doctrine, but he *did* use his authority to prevent others from imposing *their* doctrines. What one writer has described as 'a curious kind of ecclesiastical anarchy' prevailed, in which there was wide variety in the doctrine preached and in the organisation adopted.[17] This presented a peculiar challenge to Independents, Presbyterians, Erastians and Anglicans. We shall look at the response of each in turn: a response which helped to determine their subsequent fortunes, and to destroy the ideal of a 'Godly Rule'.

Cromwell's refusal to impose a coherent doctrine from the centre should have been welcome above all to Independents: if they were true to their 'sect-ideal', they should have rejoiced at the freedom to individual congregations. This is to take too simplistic a view of Independency.[18] Among Independents in the Whitehall Debates there were separatists like Goodwin, and non-separatists like Nye and Ireton. Nye, indeed, argued that the peculiar trait of Independency was its congregational and not its anti-Erastian character.[19] And during the Commonwealth those who thought like Nye – ministers such as Brow and Greenhill – accepted, or continued to hold, benefices, while others remained in a position of separation even from the Cromwellian Establishment.[20] As we have seen already, the phenomenon of a non-separating congregationalism had its roots in Elizabethan England. Moreover, while we are familiar with the way in which an ungodly ruler could inspire centrifugal tendencies in the loyal subject, we should realise also that a godly ruler could inspire *centripetal* tendencies in the sectarian. If Mary, Queen of Scots, was a provocation to a John Knox, so too in the opposite sense was an Oliver Cromwell to a John Goodwin. Brightman had argued the need for 'the setting and going apart' from the magistrate, even when the magistrate was a Christian Prince. But it is clear that Brightman did not hold the Emperor Constantine in too high esteem: for all the outward trappings of his regime 'as touching true piety, all began to waxe worse and worse'. The godly Cromwell was a much more tempting figure to the sectarian than Constantine had ever been. Moreover, this was the time when covetous glances were directed to New England: was not a *national* – as opposed to merely a *congregational* – pattern of virtue being established there? So had thought even that sober antiquarian, Simonds D'Ewes:

> Vices and sins are so severely punished amongst them, and the godly so countenanced and advanced, as in that respect it seems to be a true type of heaven itself.[21]

If ever there was a time for congregationalists to lift their eyes beyond the horizons of their congregations it was in the first years of Cromwell's rule. And, lifting their eyes, many saw Presbyterians with similar yearning after discipline and purity: here was a basis for a genuine unity. Anthony Palmer, for instance, wrote a pamphlet in 1654 to show how, in Gloucestershire, the common acceptance of the need to preserve unmixed communion was driving Presbyterian and Independent together. He expressed his gratitude to a magistrate such as Cromwell, who allowed church fellowships to form 'through common subjection to Christ, not through coercion by human power'.[22] If the Millennium was increasingly becoming the property of the propertyless, it is important to realise that the effort of Independent ministers to achieve a *rapport* with their Presbyterian colleagues was, in many cases, prompted by a millenarian impulse. As one pamphlet answered its own question – 'what then is the present interest of the Saints and people of God?' –

> To associate together into several church-societies and corporations (according to the Congregational way) till being increased and multiplied, they may combine into general assemblies or church-parliaments (according to the Presbyterian way); and then shall God give them authority and rule over the nations and kingdoms of the world. For the present to lay aside all differences and divisions amongst themselves,

and continue together against the Antichristian powers of the world (Rev. 15, 2, etc.), whom they may expect to combine against them universally (Rev. 17, 13, 14).[23]

Ultimately, hopes for unity on the basis of a pure, 'unmixed' communion foundered: John Howe wrote to Richard Baxter in May 1658 that the profession of visible faith, which Baxter required in the communicant before admitting him to the Sacrament of the Lord's Supper, still fell short of the 'deeper discoverie' which Philip Nye thought necessary: a view that was underlined by the Declaration drawn up by the Independent ministers at the Savoy Conference on 12 October 1658.[24] The bitterness that followed the failure of such efforts continued to divide Presbyterian from Independent after the Restoration, and facilitated the triumph of Anglicanism. What is important for our purpose is to realise that, after failing to achieve a real advance towards 'Godly Rule' in such favourable circumstances, most Independents were left with no alternative but to eschew more ambitious plans, and to content themselves with establishing the purity of their separate congregations after the Restoration.

The position of the Presbyterians under Cromwell is far more complex. One historian correctly saw that what killed Presbyterianism in England ultimately was the gap between theory and practice: after the Restoration, the Presbyterians clung to the ideal of a National Church while, in practice, they had more and more to conform to a sectarian position.[25] Richard Baxter named the chief culprit: the persecuting Anglicanism after the Restoration that drove Presbyterians into sectarianism:

> I think I ought to give Posterity notice, that by the Prelatists' malice, and unreasonable implacable Violence, Independency and Separation got greater advantages, against Presbytery, and all setled accidental extrinsick order and means of concord, than ever it had in these Kingdoms since the World began. . . . And Presbyterians were forced to forbear all Exercise of their way: they durst not meet together (Synodically) unless in a Gaol. . . . So that their Congregations were, through necessity, just of Independent and Separating Shape, and outward Practice, though not upon the same Principles.[26]

Baxter was being over-charitable in this explanation, both to

his co-religionists and to himself. Presbyterians had been drifting into a sectarian position long before the Restoration: this had
indeed been part of the Erastian protest in 1645 against the
claims made by Presbyterian ministers to more severe disciplinary
powers of suspension and excommunication. These claims were
rightly seen by Independents as offering the basis for an understanding with Presbyterians. The Independent, Saltmarsh, argued
that 'not mixt Communion and Fellowship, but pure and unmixt,
is the only ordinance of Christ', and his Presbyterian opponent,
Ley, replied:

> and who can tell but the purging of the Church from scandals,
> and the keeping of the Ordinances pure, when it shall be
> actually seen to be the great worke endeavoured on both sides,
> may make union betwixt us and the Independents more easie
> than many imagine.[27]

This was the view that Thomas Coleman, the leading Erastian
in the controversies, held up to ridicule:

> Sure I dreame! But I will tell you newes: the Presbyterians
> and Independents are united: nay more, the Lutherans and
> Calvinists: nay more yet, the Papists and Protestants: nay
> more than so, the Turke and Christian! But wherein? In hold-
> ing that there is a Religion wherein men ought to walke.[28]

Coleman was too serious a person to leave it as a bad joke. Ley
had acknowledged his debt to the leading Presbyterian, Gillespie,
for the insight that 'the Presbyterians and the Independents are
both equally interested against the Erastian principles'. Coleman
saw the magnitude of Gillespie's surrender:

> speaking of the efficacie and usefulnesse of Church-govern-
> ment, he gives instance in the purity of the ordinances and
> members preserved ... for an Independent to have given this
> instance, had been something; but for a Commissioner from
> Scotland, a champion for the Presbyterian Government to
> say so, seemes strange.[29]

Why was a Presbyterian such as Gillespie speaking the
language of Independency? The anarchy of Civil War and the
disappointment of the Westminster Assembly had left a vacuum
at the centre. Until such time as a 'sin-searching, sin-discovering

and sin-censuring discipline' could *truly* be established in England, *something* must be done to counter the breakdown of order. Paralysis at the centre vindicated individual attempts by the clergy to assert their disciplinary powers. Thus the motive of Presbyterians and Independents in their discussions about unity through a 'pure' communion was quite different: to the Independents this represented a widening of horizons, to the Presbyterians a shrinking. What to the Independents was a step towards a 'Godly Rule' was to Presbyterians a step away from it.

In the Civil War, the *accidental* vacuum at the centre had stimulated sectarian tendencies within Presbyterianism; in the Commonwealth, the *deliberate* vacuum at the centre produced similar effects. Thus the Independent, Anthony Palmer, could express his approval in 1654 of the greater concern to preserve the purity of the Sacraments that he had noted in the recent actions of London Presbyterian ministers. Palmer argued that, now that the situation in the Interregnum had exposed the futility of Presbyterian hopes for the achievement of purity through the sword of the civil magistrate, the chances of unity were strengthened. No accident that Palmer should cite 'learned Mr. Gillespy, in his *Aarons Rod*', and sneer at the 'Erastian' tenet of 'Church-power being in the magistrate'.[30] Palmer was reinvoking Gillespie's thesis of the natural sympathy between Presbyterian and Independent clericalism.

But there were Presbyterians who viewed with alarm the drift to sectarianism. Henry Jeanes was their most doughty apologist. The title of a pamphlet which he wrote in 1653 is itself highly revealing: *The Want of Church-Government No Warrant For a Totall Omission of the Lord's Supper*. In it Jeanes posed the vital question as to whether or not 'the Sacrament of the Lord's Supper may (according to Presbyteriall principles) be lawfully administered in an un-Presbyterated Church'. He faced the possibility that the Church of England might not become Presbyterian in his lifetime. Yet this was no ground for sectarianism. The temporary exercise of their suspending powers during Cromwell's rule by Presbyterian ministers could only reinforce the cause of separatism. He deplored them acting 'upon a principle of their own, which was never granted them by the old-Non-Conformists; to wit, that a worship is to be omitted for the sinne of the worshipers'. In an un-Presbyterated Church, the ministers have the power, only of order, not of discipline. It is no slur upon them if hypocrites enter for communion:

> this objection is taken from an Independents forge, and will not be owned by Presbyterians that understand their own Principles.[31]

But another approach altogether *was* possible for Presbyterians who understood their own principles. They could view with equanimity the chaos and lack of discipline. Indeed, they could rejoice in it – point a finger at Independency and say in effect: 'This is what happens when you don't have a proper Presbyterian discipline.' This is the attitude of one opponent of Jeanes, Fullwood. There was nothing novel in his approach. It had been the one adopted by Presbyterians in the period between 1641 and 1645: failures to implement a speedy reformation of morals were shrugged off as a consequence of a *lack* of Presbyterian discipline. But, as we have seen, even a supporter like Terry had felt that the guilt attached also to the Presbyterian ministers: a feeling which had sparked off the Erastian challenge of that time. The Presbyterian ministers were driven to take individual disciplinary action to counter the anarchy: and only succeeded in reinforcing the suspicions of the Erastians.

What *is* novel about Fullwood is that he writes as if the Erastian controversy had never happened. Most other apologists for suspension argue the need for *some* disciplinary action amidst chaos. Fullwood glories in the chaos. He believed that compliance with the civil power could only frustrate, by partial appeasement, his hopes for a real Presbyterian reformation. The doctrinaire Anglican, Hammond, interestingly sides with the doctrinaire Presbyterian, Fullwood, on this issue against Jeanes. Fullwood, who, like Hammond, was irreconcilably opposed to Cromwell, put internal purity first. Jeanes saw the slighting of the ordinances as a blow against order. Fullwood, on the other hand, welcomed

the immediate disorder as a prelude to the ultimate discipline.
This argument Jeanes deplored:

> I have proved, a command for the Lords Supper, obliging
> even in an Unpresbiterated Church; and to transgresse this
> command for this end, to stir up men's endeavours after a re-
> formation, is but a Carnall Policy: a doing of evill that good
> may come.[32]

Jeanes – counselling against a 'doing of evill that good may come'
– sounds very like Cromwell when he warned that it 'is not enough
to propose things that are good in the end'. Both, in their concern
about means rather than ends, seem to typify a general attitude.
Only rarely does a doctrinaire voice – a Fullwood, a Hammond –
speak. Engels had shocked the pragmatic English Chartist,
Harney, by his welcome to the virtual destruction of the Ten
Hours Bill in 1850:

> Working men of England, if you, your wives, and children
> are again to be locked up in the 'rattle boxes' for thirteen hours
> a day, do not despair. This is a cup which, though bitter, must
> be drunk. The sooner you get over it, the better. Your proud
> masters, be assured, have dug their grave in obtaining what
> they call a victory over you.[33]

Men with an apocalyptic vision, confident of ultimate truths,
could swallow penultimate lies. The taste might be bitter, but the
cup must be drunk. Men, less confident of ends, more concerned
about consequences, were not convinced that the cup *must* be
drunk. Most apologists for suspension on the Presbyterian side
argued for these powers, not as Fullwood did, to sabotage the
authority of the civil power, but in order to buttress it.

Why should Presbyterians aid Cromwell? The answer is given
most clearly by Richard Baxter. We have already noted his gratitude to the Protector for the moral good achieved by the Triers.
And although he had no great affection for Cromwell, he gener-
ously praised him for the liberty that he was given to preach
the Gospel 'under an usurper whom I opposed'. Baxter would
have liked a 'Godly Rule', but there were advantages in setting
one's sights lower:

> I think that land most happy whose rulers use their authority

for Christ as well as for the civil peace, yet in comparison of the rest of the world I still think that land happy that hath but bare liberty to be as good as they are willing to be.[34]

Yet gratitude could slide imperceptibly into pusillanimity. We see this in an apology for 'pure communion' from a Presbyterian, Humphrey Saunders, in 1655. Saunders indicated his disapproval of sedition 'while the present authority is for us (at least not against us), and we no underminers of them, nor are we tumultuous, or injurious'. Saunders spoke the language of Munich:

> we constraine none. . . . If we cannot convince, and satisfie other mens consciences, we leave them to themselves.[35]

That a Presbyterian could see this as a cause for self-congratulation, rather than for soul-searching, indicated to opponents of unmixed communion how far Presbyterianism had lost its proselytising urge, and had taken on a sectarian colouring in the Interregnum.

Baxter was in a difficult position. Cromwell might be an usurper whom he opposed, but how far was obedience to be denied to a ruler who did not try to open windows into men's souls; who indeed showed a laudable concern to deal with moral failings? This was the question that John Wilson posed in a letter to Baxter, when he expressed doubts about whether Presbyterians should support Booth's rising. Wilson was haunted by the precepts of Bucer, Calvin and Pareus against active resistance to 'even a meer possessory power'.[36] Baxter attempted to steer a 'middle way', as he put it himself, during the Commonweath: neither to work so fervently with the ruling power as to seem to condone his title, nor to sabotage the ruling power so as to cause a breakdown in government. The Worcestershire Association, which Baxter formed, reflected the confusion: to a supporter of mixed communion, like Humfrey, its basis of admission to the Sacrament seemed too narrow, too like that of the Independents;[37] to Independents, however, it fell short of the 'deeper discoverie' that they thought was necessary. John Bryan wrote to Baxter, querying whether the minister should continue to withhold the Sacrament from his parishioners in Shrewsbury. He pointed out that it was a large parish, with many ignorant persons, and that ministers in country districts were generally more exacting than those in towns. Much as Baxter abhorred the neglect of the Sacrament, he could not but approve of the minister's search for 'order and decencye'.[38] Yet the ideal of an 'unmixed communion' was of profound embarrassment to many Presbyterians, as one correspondent made clear to Baxter in 1658:

> A younger brother of Colonel Birch did in much haste urge it, That wee must invite and take in (as far as wee could obtaine it) all the Ministers into this Association; or we did in effect judge them that were not received, scandalous or insufficient.[39]

Despite the tremendous contribution that Presbyterians made to the Restoration of Charles II, their failure to sustain a grip on the Establishment becomes more intelligible against the background of tensions and hesitations that marked their cause in the Commonwealth. Drifting into a sectarian position, flirting with Independents (so that a vicious Anglican like L'Estrange could make debating points out of the fact that they always did things together, and thus put the blame for Charles I's death on their hands), uneasy about the extent of their allegiance to the *de facto* ruler, the Presbyterians were in poor psychological shape at the end of the Commonwealth to exploit to the full the military advantages wrested for them by Monk. So too – and to some extent for similar reasons – were many Anglicans. But not, as we shall see, the 'Laudians' – the residual victors of the struggles for power between 1658 and 1661.

The Erastians seemed, of all the groups in the Commonwealth, least affected by change. Prynne, Humfrey, Morice, Timson, Blake – these were the men who continued the arguments of Coleman for 'mixed communion' against clerical disciplinary power. But there was a crucial difference between the Erastian position in the 1640s and in the 1650s. In the 1640s the Erastians had not been concerned with exalting Parliament: we saw that this this was a libel, cleverly fathered on them by their Presbyterian opponents. Yet they still assumed that the civil authority, the Long Parliament, would carry out the moral reforms which they were agitating for. This assumption was no longer tenable. In the centre was now a vacuum. Erastian writers, as different from each other as were Prynne, Humfrey and Louis du Moulin, all agreed on one thing: that if the clerical claims to disciplinary power were still unjustified, they nevertheless had a plausibility that they had lacked in the 1640s.[40] The Presbyterian ministers, and their Independent colleagues, were only filling the vacuum created by a ruler who would not play Constantine. Would there not be anarchy if the ministers did not exercise disciplinary powers?

There was only one answer to this, and this was one that all the Erastians made. No longer did they advance, even in passing, the proposition that the civil power should effect moral reforms. What they said was that moral reforms were advanced by a policy of common admission to the Sacraments and were held back by a policy of exclusion from the Sacraments. Prynne and other Erastians had turned to the civil magistrate in 1645 to wield the sovereign powers that the 'root and branch' ministers – with the exception of those in London – had proved unfit to wield. Now, when nothing could be expected from the civil magistrate, something had to be done. The Sacrament of the Lord's Supper must continue to be administered, preaching must go on. Prynne had made his position clear on that point as early as January 1648. Then he had delivered a blistering attack upon the Standing Committee for Somerset for prosecuting a former Cavalier minister, Tanner, thus leaving 'three parishes together, like sheep without a shepherd, quite destitute of all spiritual food for their souls'. Prynne stated the true order of priorities:

> in time of scarcity of ministers there is a necessity of admitting such, though they have been against us, rather than people should want ministers to instruct them.[41]

And Prynne pointed out that Archbishop Usher had been found acceptable, although he had served with the King, 'upon these grounds, that his doctrine is orthodox and pious, and his life blameless'.[42]

It was a moral impulse that had moved such men to look to the civil authority in 1645; when no action could be expected from the civil authority, the moral impulse remained. Until the time of the Commonwealth, Prynne had accepted the view of his great Jacobean predecessor, Robert Bolton, that 'take Sovereignty from the face of the earth, and you turne it into a Cockpit'. In the novel situation of the Commonwealth, Prynne began to have second thoughts about the need for sovereignty. He recognised that magistrates *ought* to be like Gods, but at the same time knew that there was 'a strange corrupting transforming venom... in sovereign powers and dignities'. He vowed in future, 'not greedily or arbitrarily to seek after Empire, Sovereignty, Power, Magistracy'. And he who had once sought for the vengeful sword of Jehovah now believed that no quality was more precious in the Christian Magistrate than a compassionate integrity.[43] Hating Cromwell, Prynne was subtly transformed by him: it is thus less surprising that he should end his days at the feet of a Latitudinarian bishop.[44]

Prynne makes an interesting contrast with Fullwood here. Fullwood had been in favour of the suspending power in Presbyterian ministers as an instrument of *disorder*. The immediate disorder was the preliminary to the ultimate discipline. In political matters Prynne's position was no different. He was as keen on a restored monarchy as Fullwood on a restored Presbyterianism. He was ready to provoke immediate political disorders – we know of his complicity in Royalist conspiracies in the Interregnum – in order to make men eager for the order and discipline of a restored monarchy. When it came to ecclesiastical matters there was a stop in Prynne's mind. He could not view with Fullwood's complacency the breakdown of moral order, because moral order remained as the *forefront* of his thoughts. This had been apparent as early in 1645 when Gillespie's sophisticated explanations for the failure hitherto of Presbyterianism to create a 'Godly Rule' in England were so patently lost on Prynne. With a divine simplicity Prynne kept coming back to the central point: the ministers had promised a swift reformation of morals and they had not honoured that promise.

John Locke once said that 'it is of great use to the sailor to know the length of his line' even although 'he cannot with it fathom all the depths of the ocean'. The Commonwealth was a great time for drawing in lines: for measuring what was there, rather than speculating about what might be there. Ends had become identified with millenarian speculation; millenarian speculation had become identified with egalitarianism and crankiness. This was the time when men such as Baxter preferred to forget the importance they had once attached to the Apocalypse. But we have seen that Prynne, like Baxter, showed a new willingness at this time to eschew ends and concentrate on means. Why, then, did they quarrel – and so bitterly that Humfrey, on Prynne's behalf, was to chide Baxter in a private letter for his ability to cut his opponents to the heart, instead of pinching them *at* the heart?[45] Prynne, of course, was the last person to need defence from invective. Why the two quarrelled was because they agreed on the need for minimum disciplinary measures to be taken in the face of moral anarchy, but disagreed profoundly about what *discipline* was. To Baxter it was the rigorous scrutiny of candidates for admission to the Sacraments; to Prynne, it was the opposite. When Prynne saw men refusing to attend the Sacrament, and ministers refusing to administer it, he called explicitly for a revival of the 'Godly Discipline' of the past.[46] Yet their quarrel must not blind us to their fundamental agreement: neither believed that the measures they proposed were *in themselves* a 'Godly Rule'; they were only interim police action. Both had given up the task of fathoming all the depths of the ocean.

So too had many Anglicans in the Commonwealth. Modern research has not supported the claims to martyrdom made by large numbers of Anglican clergy at the Restoration.[47] Under Cromwell they suffered persecution if they were identified with political dissidence; otherwise, true to his *laissez-faire* policy, they were permitted considerable freedom of worship at *parish level*. And many seized the opportunity. Their leading apologist was Robert Sanderson, who argued that disobedience to the *de facto* ruler was a failure in duty: 'And surely it argueth a most perverse mind, to be willing to live under the protection of his Government, whom you are unwilling to obey.'[48] Brian Duppa said: 'I secure myself the same way as the tortoise doth, by not going out of my shell.' And Duppa – as we know from his correspondence with Isham – was one of the more active bishops in the Commonwealth. Many Anglicans followed Duppa in a 'tortoise' policy. In a curiously inverted way, they were now taking on the mantle of non-separating congregationalism. The danger soon for Anglicanism in the Commonwealth was not extirpation through persecution but collapse through senescence. For the bishops were dying out: by 1659 only nine bishops were left – in ages ranging from 67 to 78. The survivors were lamentably timid about filling the gap. As Clarendon said at the time, if he were a Presbyterian negotiator he would 'spin out the time till all the Bishops were dead'.[49]

It is against this background that the activities of those who would not let themselves be assimilated should be assessed. The term 'Laudian' was applied to this group by Dr Bosher, who has made a most important study of their activities. He realised that it was an unsatisfactory term in many ways:[50] Sheldon was no intimate of Laud, he abandoned the financial independence of the Church in 1664, and he never attempted to revive the Church courts and disciplinary powers, and with it the social policy of his predecessor. The term would be less misleading if we were content to sum up Laudianism in the sycophancy of a Mainwaring or a Sibthorpe. But this we cannot do. As we have seen, the whole idea of 'Laudianism' was bound up with the disciplinary role of the Church. This Sheldon never attempted to revive. Some historians have credited Sheldon with the authorship of a tract which referred to 'that most damnable and heretical doctrine of the Church of Rome, whore of Babylon', and which warned that the King might draw upon himself 'Gods heavy wrath and indignation'.[51] We know now that this is bad history: that the tract was written some forty years earlier, possibly by Archbishop Abbott.[52] But, even without this knowledge, the attribution is bad psychology. Sheldon – who denied at his doctoral examination that the Pope was Antichrist – was not the man to use that sort of language. Abbott might have done. His case is not so psychologically implausible. This seems at first sight strange: Abbott was not renowned for any great pastoral sense of vocation. But because Abbott had been too lazy and unenergetic to will the *means* of a 'Godly Rule' it does not follow that he rejected the *ends* of a 'Godly Rule': there is a huge gap between the *unconscious* Latitudinarianism of an easy-going clergyman like Abbott and the *conscious* Latitudinarianism of a post-Restoration clergyman like Tillotson. Laud differed from Abbott not in *ends* but in the energy with which he pursued the *means*. Laud and his associates could share Foxe's millenarian vision, though not his regard for the Godly Prince. Downame had seen the Godly Church as a body fighting precisely the same enemy as Foxe's Godly Prince: the Church of Rome which was 'the whore of Babylon, the see of Antichrist';[53] Mountague still thought of the papacy as *an* Antichrist, if not *the* Antichrist; Cosin had thought of the Turk as Antichrist.

Laud's successors at the Restoration dropped that sort of language. On the other hand, Sancroft, Allestree and Clark revived Laud's claims for a divine right episcopacy in sermons after the Restoration.[54] Opponents professed to be greatly alarmed about such claims. Zachary Crofton anticipated Dr Bosher by some three hundred years by referring to these clergymen, in a pamphlet of 1661, as 'the *Laudenses* of our Age'.[55] He warmly welcomed the action taken by William Prynne in that year in republishing one of his most eloquent pamphlets against *iure divino* claims for episcopacy.[56] The pamphlet had first been written in 1636. Prynne's action underlined Crofton's point: 1636 or 1661 – what did it matter? Laudianism had been restored.

Prynne never totally relaxed his vigilance. A *iure divino* claim for episcopacy was always enough to set the old Puritan bloodhound sniffing for traces of Laudianism: this was true up to his death in 1669. But it was also true that, by that time, he had largely made his peace with Anglicanism: Tillotson at the end of Prynne's life was as acceptable a bishop to him as Jewel had been at the beginning of his life. If the Restoration Church had in reality been Laudian Prynne could not have made his peace with it.

The resemblances indeed *were* superficial. Sancroft, Allestree and Clark might borrow Laudian language in defending *iure divino* claims for bishops, but that was all that they borrowed. In the writings of the Jacobean divines the claims had been a conscious philosophical challenge to the dangerous Tudor emphasis on the powers of the civil magistrate. William Barlow put it pithily: 'But RELIGION turned into STATISME, will soon prove ATHEISME.'[57] Barlow, and Laud after him, made the *iure divino* claim the basis for their plea for the supremacy of the Godly Bishop. The *iure divino* claim had a very different significance for those who made it in the Commonwealth and after the Restoration. It was not a proud assertion of *supremacy*, but, rather, a desperate plea for *survival*. The question that Cromwell's non-rule had posed for Anglicanism in the Interregnum was whether it was to survive as an organised movement of opposition (like Popish recusancy before it), or as a point of view, influencing from within (like 'old nonconformity' before it). Hammond argued the first, Sanderson argued the second. Those who sided with Hammond would have no truck with the Protector and welcomed, as warmly as the doctrinaire Presbyterian, Fullwood, had done, the prospects of a breakdown of public order. Hammond and others like him – Morley, Gunning, Cosin, Ferne and Earle – were glad to borrow the Laudian argument that Anglicanism continued to exist by divine right. In the context of so much compliance at parish level – we know that even Sheldon did not sever his links with his Buckinghamshire parish until as late as 1650[58] – and so little leadership at the top from the surviving bishops, this stand won for 'Laudians' the support of all those who wished to see Anglicanism restored as the dominant force in the ecclesiastical life of the nation. Yet this did not mean that they wished to see that position used for ends that Laud would have approved of: only in this limited sense can Clarendon, for instance, be called a 'Laudian'.[59] While the issue was one of the *political survival* of Anglicanism, he was a Laudian – striving with Barwick and Allestree to rouse the surviving bishops from their near-fatal apathy. When the issue was one of the *use* to which Anglicans could put their supremacy, Clarendon was more faithful to his old anti-clerical prejudices of the 1630s (when he was one of the Tew Circle that included Falkland, Hales, Chillingworth and peripherally Hobbes), than he was prepared to own up to in his highly misleading memoirs. In the tactical situation of the Interregnum period and immediately after the Restoration, the *iure divino* claim for episcopacy was a condition of its survival rather than the badge of theocracy. The difference between Sheldon's rule and Laud's is striking. As one commentator put it: 'For the first time it was admitted that she (the Restoration Church of England) did not command a monopoly of all Protestant believers in England, and whereas Laud had always endeavoured to coerce the Puritans into conformity and obedience, Sheldon simply rejected them.'[60] The 'unity of Jerusalem' was now an empty shibboleth.

'Godly Rule' was about power, and about the ethical use to which that power could be put. In the Interregnum, in their very different ways, Presbyterians, Independents, Erastians and many Anglicans were taking on a sectarian colouring. Cromwell was educating them to a different view of their responsibilities: one that put more stress on the private gesture than on the public discipline; that looked for reform from individual actions rather than from a central authority. We have now seen that even the group most outside the Cromwellian consensus, the Laudian Anglicans, were less outside it than it would appear from the *iure divino* claims that they made for episcopacy. This was their method of attaining power, but once they had obtained that power they did not use it to revive Laud's dreams of a coerced virtue. As much as their opponents they sought ethical reforms in personal actions: Archbishop Sheldon remonstrated with Charles II on his moral behaviour, but did not revive the Church courts. Men no longer believed in a Millennium – the pursuit of Utopian *ends* was now the prerogative of the crank – but they were passionately concerned about the *means* by which objectives were attained. We must now try to understand how this change had come about.

1. A. S. P. Woodhouse, ed., *Puritanism and Liberty*, pp. 474–7.

2. Ibid., p. 478.

3. Thomas Carlyle, *Oliver Cromwell's Letter and Speeches*, I, p. 187.

4. Walzer, *Revolution of the Saints*, p. 13.

5. Ibid., p. 230.

6. Woodhouse, *Puritanism and Liberty*, pp. 101–4.

7. Ibid., p. 8. My italics.

8. Carlyle, *Oliver Cromwell . . .*, III, p. 287.

9. Ibid, III 246; II 187; III 295.

10. Walzer, *Revolution of the Saints*, p. 298.

11. At almost the same time as Owen was decrying the idea of prescribing a godly pattern for rule on earth, a New England divine, Edward Johnson, was making clear just how much this represented an abandonment of New Model Army millenarianism. Johnson awaits the fall of Antichrist: with the help of inspired interpreters, like John Cotton, he expects 'some sudden blow to be given to this bloodthirsty monster'. The whole passage could have been taken from Cromwell at Marston Moor, with one important difference. There is a recognition now that a vaunted 'Godly Rule', which yet allows religious toleration to antinomian sects, is a self-contradiction. Johnson says: '*Familists, Seekers, Antinomians* and *Anabaptists*, they are so ill armed that they think it best sleeping in a whole skin, fearing that if the day of battel once go on, they shall fall among Antichrists Armies: and therefore cry out like cowards, If you will let me alone, and I will let you alone; but assuredly the Lord Christ hath said, *He that is not with us, is against us*: there is no room in his Army for toleratorists' (*The Puritans*, ed. P. Miller and T. Johnson, I 160). It is impossible not to see this as a thrust against the Cromwell of the 1650s.

12. Tuveson, *Millennium and Utopia*, p. 87

13. Perry Miller, 'Roger Williams: His Contribution to the American Tradition', *Roger Williams and the Massachusetts Magistrates* (Boston, Heath, 1964) p. 99.

14. Carlyle, *Oliver Cromwell . . .*, IV 59. Cromwell now argued that his motive in accepting office had been 'not so much out of hope of doing any good, as out of a desire to prevent mischief and evil': an astonishing reversal of what Foxe and Brightman had seen as the function of the ruler.

15. Ibid. III 294–5.

16. Richard Baxter, *Autobiography*, p. 71.

17. Anne Whiteman, 'The Restoration of the Church of

England', in *From Uniformity to Unity 1662–1962,* ed. G. F. Nuttall and O. Chadwick (London, S.P.C.K., 1962) p. 28.

18. (Public Record Office) S.P. 16/503, f. 35: an important letter of November 1644 from Godfrey to Prynne, in which he complains of this facile definition of Independency.

19. Woodhouse, *Puritanism and Liberty,* pp. 154–9; D. Nobbs, 'Philip Nye on Church and State', *Cambridge Historical Journal,* v (1935) 55; G. Yule, *The Independents in the English Civil War* (Cambridge U.P., 1958) pp. 17–18.

20. G. F. Nuttall, 'The First Nonconformists', in Nuttall and Chadwick (eds) *From Uniformity . . .,* p. 169.

21. Simonds D'Ewes, *Autobiography and Correspondence,* ed. J. O. Halliwell (London, Bentley, 1845) II 116.

22. Anthony Palmer, *A Scripture-Rule to the Lord's Table . . .* (London, 1654) p. 3.

23. Woodhouse, *Puritanism and Liberty,* p. 245.

24. (Doctor Williams's Library) Baxter MSS. 59.3., f. 196; Benjamin Hanbury, *Historical Memorials* (London, Fisher, 1844) III 525–6.

25. C. E. Whiting, *Studies in English Puritanism from the Restoration to the Revolution, 1660–88* (London, S.P.C.K., 1931) p. 46.

26. Quoted by R. Thomas, 'Comprehension and Indulgence', in Nuttall and Chadwick (eds), *From Uniformity . . .,* p. 205.

27. John Saltmarsh, *The Opening of Master Prynnes New Book . . .* (London, 1645) p. 37; John Ley, *The New Querie . . .* (London, 1645) p. 65.

28. Thomas Coleman, *A Brotherly Examination Re-examined . . .* p. 6.

29. Ibid., p. 9. Cf. George Gillespie, *Nihil Respondis . . .,* p. 18.

30. Palmer, *A Scripture-Rule . . .,* pp. 5, 7, 21, 40.

31. Henry Jeanes, *The Want of Church-Government No Warrant for a Totall Omission of the Lord's Supper* (Oxford, 1653) pp. 1, 15, 29, 145.

32. Henry Jeanes, *The Examiner Examined . . .* (Oxford, 1653) p. 250; Henry Hammond, *The Grounds of Uniformity* (London, 1657) *passim.*

33. Quoted in A. R. Schoyen, *The Chartist Challenge* (London, Heinemann, 1958) p. 205.

34. Baxter, *Autobiography,* p. 80.

35. Humphrey Saunders, *An Anti-Diatribe . . .* (London, 1655) pp. 73, 88, 116, 117.

36. (Doctor Williams's Library) Baxter MSS. 59.1, f. 261.

37. (Doctor Williams's Library) Baxter MSS. 59.1, ff. 196–7.

38. (Doctor Williams's Library) Baxter MSS. 59.1, f. 253.

39. (Doctor Williams's Library) Baxter MSS. 59.1, f. 247.

40. Louis du Moulin, *The Power of the Christian Magistrate in Sacred Things* ... (London, 1650) pp. 84–5; Prynne, *A Legal Resolution of Two Important Queries* ... (London, 1656) p. 16; John Humfrey, *An Humble Vindication of a Free Admission Unto the Lords-Supper* ... (London, 1653) p. 31.

41. Henry Cary, *Memorials of the Great Civil War in England from 1642 to 1652* (London, Colburn, 1842) I 373–4. See also the Committee's outraged reply: (Bodleian Library) Tanner MSS. 58, f. 687.

42. Henry Cary, *Memorials of the Great Civil War* ..., p. 374. Cf. Prynne, *A New Discovery of Some Romish Emissaries* ... (London, 1656) pp. 28–31. He deplored the Declaration of 24 November 1655, which prohibited ex-Cavalier ministers, 'though never so orthodox, learned, pious, painfull, from preaching, administering the Sacraments, or keeping a school'. He attacked such 'uncharitable, unchristian, unevangelical restraints'; in particular their application to Dr Reeves, the Lecturer at Lincoln's Inn, and spoke of the 'earnest frequent solicitations of devout and learned Archbishop Usher (to the shortning of his days through grief, as some conceive)'. Usher died at the age of seventy-five.

43. Prynne, *A New Discovery of Free-State Tyranny* ... (London, 1655) pp. 66–70.

44. Prynne bequeathed his *An Exact Chronologicall History* ... to Bishop Tillotson: see *Documents Relating To Proceedings against William Prynne* (Camden Society, New Series, XVIII) p. 98.

45. (Doctor Williams's Library) Baxter MSS. 59.1, f. 191.

46. Prynne, *An Appendix to a Seasonable Vindication of Free-Admission* ..., p. 9. Cf. John Humfrey, *A Second Vindication* ... (London, 1656) p. 109: 'An Orthodox Free-Admission, the end whereof is to advance discipline, not depose it.'

47. A. G. Matthews, *Walker Revised* (Oxford University Press, 1948) *passim*; R. S. Bosher, *The Making of the Restoration Settlement* (London, Black, 1951) *passim*.

48. Robert Sanderson, *Several Cases of Conscience Discussed* ... (London, 1660) p. 170.

49. Quoted by Anne Whiteman, 'The Church of England Restored', in Nuttall and Chadwick (eds) *From Uniformity* ..., p. 48.

50. Bosher, *The Making of the Restoration Settlement*, p. xv.

51. O. Airy, 'Notes on the Reign of Charles II', *British Quarterly Review*, LXXVII (1880) 332–3. This attribution is accepted –

and repeated – in G. R. Abernathy, jun., 'Clarendon and the Declaration of Indulgence', *Journal of Ecclesiastical History*, XI 1 (1960) 67.

52. F. Higham, 'Note on Gilbert Sheldon', *Journal of Ecclesiastical History*, XLV 2 (1963) 209–12.

53. Downame, *Two Sermons* (London, 1608) preface.

54. William Sancroft, *A Sermon* ... (London, 1661) p. 2; Richard Allestree, *A Sermon* ... (London, 1661) p. 13; Samuel Clark, *Ministers Dues and Peoples Duty* ... (London, 1661) pp. 3, 8, 24, 25, 26.

55. Zachary Crofton, *A Serious Review of Presbyters Re-ordination by Bishops* (London, 1661) p. 15.

56. *The Unbishoping of Timothy and Titus*. An Anglican thought that the republishing of this pamphlet was a key work in an insincere Presbyterian campaign after the Restoration against the *iure divino* claim for bishops: 'this was only to trouble the waters, and keep men irresolved as to the publick constitutions; while they confirmed the brethren in their private opinions, and are unbishoping Timothy and Titus, bidding men beware of Diotrophes, and those that Lord it over God's heritage' (Oliver Foulis, *Cabala* ... (London, 1664) p. 52).

57. William Barlow, *An Answer to a Catholike Englishman* (London, 1609) p. 370.

58. Anne Whiteman, 'The Church of England Restored', in Nuttall and Chadwick (eds), *From Uniformity* ..., p. 36.

59. The two most important *critiques* of Dr Bosher's identification of Clarendon with his 'Laudian' group are: (implicitly) B. H. G. Wormald, *Clarendon: Politics, History and Religion, 1640–1660* (Cambridge University Press, 1951); (explicitly) G. R. Abernathy, jun., 'Clarendon and the Declaration of Indulgence', *Journal of Ecclesiastical History* XI 1 (1960) 55–73.

60. Kenyon, *The Stuart Constitution*, p. 364.

7 Ends and Means

> This propaganda of beneficence, this constant attention
> to the moral and physical improvement of persons who
> have been neglected, is quite recent as a leading feature
> of religion, though indeed it seems to have formed some
> part of the Saviour's original design. It was unknown to
> the great preachers of the seventeenth century, whether
> Catholic or Puritan, and it offered but a shadowy attrac-
> tion to my Father, who was the last of their disciples.[1]

We have already seen why Edmund Gosse was right to see his
Victorian father as the last of the seventeenth-century Puritans.
When Edmund Gosse, as a young man, went alone to London
for the first time his father badgered him with a constant flow of
letters. But the anxiety that his father expressed in these letters
was not about his moral behaviour – the vulnerability of an innocent youth exposed to the temptations of London – but about
the intellectual part of his son's faith. As Gosse put it: 'these
incessant exhortations dealt, not with conduct, but with faith', In
this, as in so many other ways, the Victorian millenarian captured
the authentic spirit of seventeenth-century Protestantism. *Means*
do not matter if the *ends* are right; we discover *ends* from Scripture, above all from the Book of Revelation.

By 1660 these assumptions are no longer widely tenable. This
is clear from the Declaration of Breda that Charles II published
in that year. This was his declaration of intent; his message to his
people before returning to the throne. Historians have given it
short shrift: at best, it is flabby; at worst, disingenuous. If there
ever were a real charitable aim in religious matters, Breda was
swiftly dishonoured by the persecution of dissent in the Clarendon Code. So there are good reasons for ignoring it. And yet, as

a record of aspiration, it deserves a closer scrutiny. Take the passage on religion:

> And because the passion and uncharitableness of the times have produced several opinions in religion, by which men are engaged in parties and animosities against each other, which, when they shall hereafter unite in a freedom of conversation, will be composed and better understood, we do declare a liberty for tender consciences, and that no man shall be disquieted or called in question for differences of opinion in matters of religion which do not disturb the peace of the kingdom; and that we shall be ready to consent to such an act of parliament as, upon mature deliberation, shall be offered to us, for the full granting that indulgence.[2]

What is missing in this passage? Any conviction that the return of the Christian Emperor, and of a united Church, will lead to moral regeneration (as opposed to peace and good order). In a document teeming with platitudes, the one great platitude from the first half of the century is absent.

It is in this sense that the Clarendon Code fulfils, not betrays, the Declaration of Breda. A 'Code' is what it is not. Men were searching for a code before the Restoration: for laws and regulations that enforced virtuous living. No such spirit informs the Clarendon Code, which is merely a series of *ad hoc* punitive measures. The victims could be forgiven for assuming that Laudianism had been reincarnated; especially since many of their persecutors shared this delusion. But in Laud's time the Church of England could plausibly speak for the nation; those who dissented were disrupters of the unity of Jerusalem. This could not be argued with a straight face after the experiences of Anglicans in the Interregnum. Once the Church of England had lost its comprehensive position its authority to effect a 'Godly Rule' was undermined. But if the Civil War and its aftermath provided a *long-term* justification for toleration, it provided a *short-term* justification for intolerance by identifying religious dissent with sedition. Bishop Cosin's apology for persecution after the Restoration was: 'Let us be sheep and be sure they will not be wolves.' Did he really believe this? Sincere or not, his admission marks a striking change from the time of Laud. Laud saw himself as neither sheep nor wolf, but shepherd. Cosin lacked this pastoral sense of purpose, although he had been formerly an intimate of Laud. This sense of drift is perceptible throughout the Clarendon Code; self-preservation is the key. The problem is not how to convey truths to make men better but how to construct laws to make them safer. Now safety was subject to an empirical investigation in the way that an ethical aspiration was not. Charles II's effort to halt persecution in 1672 was prefaced with the words: 'It being evident by the sad experience of twelve years that there is very little fruit of all these forcible courses.' Laud was no sadist: there is no evidence that he was gratified by the brutal punishments inflicted on opponents such as Prynne, Burton and Bastwick in 1637. But neither was he deflected from his course by the violent emotions aroused by the slicing off of their ears. He did not *expect* to see fruit of his forcible courses. His diary reflects no remorse or disquiet about the merit of his actions. As much as his Puritan opponents, he communicates in his diary an unwavering conviction in the rectitude of his ends. Like them, he combines this with anxiety about the means he has adopted. But his criterion is whether they have advanced the 'Godly Rule' that they were meant to serve; and this is not necessarily measured by the godliness of the individual action. In Arthur Koestler's novel, *Darkness at Noon*, the Marxist prisoner, Rubashov, writes in his diary:

> The ultimate truth is penultimately always a falsehood. He who will be proved right in the end appears to be wrong and harmful before it.

As belief in an ultimate truth recedes, concern about penultimate falsehood swells. A public code cannot make men moral; then the onus is the greater on the individual. For this reason, Burnet's sneer at Laud's successor, Archbishop Sheldon, was unworthy: 'a wise and honest clergyman, that had little virtue and less religion'. This was an unfair verdict on a man who was prepared to stand up to Charles II on the question of his morality, but more than that it misses the essential point about the Restoration Church: personal virtue was the *only* answer to immorality once reliance on a disciplinary code had been undermined. Sheldon dropped Laud's social policy, and in 1664 renounced the claim of the Church to tax itself and with it the possibility of its passing a policy unsupported by Parliament; yet he would not receive a mistress of Charles II in his lodgings. These were not self-contradictory actions; the one was a necessary consequence of the other. Virtue was now an end in itself, not a means to an end. The low-powered emphasis of Restoration divines on personal morality is well mirrored in Tillotson's words: 'The great business of religion is to make men truly good and to teach them to live well.' Not for these men the creation of disciplinary courts, a Westminster Assembly or a Court of High Commission; instead, if they were a Patrick or a Tenison, they built charity schools. There was the assumption not only that virtue was attainable through personal actions but that it was *only* attainable through those channels. Bishop Burnet was only joking in 1675 when he said that there were two sorts of persons that ought not to meddle in public matters: churchmen and women. 'We ought to be above it, and women were below it,' was his comfortable reflection. Underlying the joke, however, were some revealing preconceptions; most notably the belief that churchmen lost virtue by intervening in politics. In the earlier period an anti-clerical lawyer like John Selden would have enjoyed the joke hugely, but not most of the writers in the 1640s who were unhelpfully bracketed with him as 'Erastians' and who, as we have seen, in fact shared the ideal of 'Godly Rule' with Laudian and Presbyterian. One of these was William Prynne, and the change in him after the Restoration was striking. It was not a change of principle but a change of aspiration. He continued to believe that reform should come through the civil magistrate, but the kind of reform that interested him in the sixties was shown by his speeches in the Commons against absenteeism and pluralism, and in favour of the building of more churches. Twenty years earlier he had been looking to the sword of the Christian Emperor to inflict capital punishment on 'Blasphemous and execrable Cursers and Swearers'. Prynne paid Tillotson the compliment of bequeathing one of his turgid, unreadable volumes to him in his will: the Calvinist zealot ended up at the feet of a Latitudinarian divine.

Swift detected a parallel development with Quakerism: 'from a system of religion first founded upon enthusiasm it had developed into a craft'. In the retreat from 'Godly Rule' the Quakers play a doubly significant role. First, they offered the doctrinal challenge to Calvinism that Laud had evaded. They denied the rigid Calvinist doctrine of election; by attention to the preaching of the inner light the individual could save himself. This had its dangers, as when Naylor, the Quaker, believed that he was the Messiah. Samuel Parker, another influential writer in the period after the Restoration, argued that 'all religion must of necessity be resolved into Enthusiasm or Morality'; George Fox drew the same moral for the Quakers. So successfully did he apply it that Richard Baxter, who was no friend of the Quakers, marvelled at the way they had changed under the influence of Fox from 'horrid profaneness and blasphemy to a life of extreme austerity'.[3] Burnet's quip they took seriously, and politics was something not to be meddled with. Their one serious diversion from this principle – when Penn persuaded some of them to support Algernon Sidney in the election of 1681 – was a disaster that discouraged repetition. The second achievement of the Quakers was their stout-heartedness in the face of persecution. There were some Quakers, such as Wilkinson and Story, who were so attached to the ideas of personal responsibility and so suspicious of corporate discipline that they defended the practice of fleeing in times of persecution, because the custom not to flee had hardened into an unwritten law! Fortunately for the cause of religious toleration they remained a minority. Men who led godly lives were being persecuted on political pretexts that were becoming less and less plausible.

But worse: they were being punished for refusing to testify to what they believed to be false. As Comrade Rubashov, in Koestler's novel, comes to realise: 'the ultimate truth always receded a step; visible remained only the penultimate lie with which one had to serve it'. Men who doubted an ultimate truth – as Locke said, 'in this great variety of ways that men follow, it is still doubtful which is the right one' – were not prepared to swallow the penultimate lie. Truth mattered: the power of religion came from the inward and full persuasion of the mind. Hence the futility of compulsion: 'no religion which I believe not to be true can be either true or profitable unto me', said Locke.

There is a stereotype of the Puritan: of an upright Daniel, of unshakeable integrity and candour, whose word is his bond. Such a person may have existed in the first half of the seventeenth century (and if he did, he may have looked a little like William Prynne), but if so one meets him very rarely. Men hungering for 'Godly Rule' took lightly the scruples that haunted Locke; could a revolution be conducted according to the rules of cricket? Locke, the stern umpire, said: 'Yes.' His general approval of the principle of toleration did not stretch as far as Roman Catholics, atheists and antinomian sects. Why? Because they were equivocators, who regarded no promise or oath as binding. The antinomianism that Locke had in mind was of sects like the Ranters, of whom one critic said:

> They use to speake one thinge and mean another . . . . They will say and unsay in one breath . . . . They will smile upon you, and cut your throate: use melting words, *Honeysweet,* smoothe as oyle, but full of poyson.[4]

The Ranters carried the Calvinist denial of personal merit to its logical, if perverted, conclusion. Yet almost all Puritans before 1660 were touched with this spirit. In his analysis of the debates within the Roundhead Army during the Civil War, Dr Woodhouse noted in the Puritan mind 'a rather obscure tendency . . . to regard no bargain as binding once it has ceased to be advantageous – especially to the children of grace'.[5] This made it easier for Puritans to develop the thesis of 'progressive comprehension' both as the explanation for a change of front, and its justification. Such flexibility made them slippery enemies for a persecutor to track down, and prompted a cry of anguish from one would-be persecutor to Laud in 1638:

> John Fathers, clerk, vicar of St. Stephen's, Cornwall, having committed offences punishable by the High Commission Court, has reported that if any question him he shall lose his

labour, for that upon appearance he will confess, and then he shall be dismissed; and so he reports that Prynne and Bastwick might have been, if they would have recanted, and thereby he deters every one from prosecuting him.[6]

The redoubtable John Fathers, the more redoubtable for eschewing romantic gestures, stood for all who put 'Godly Rule' above godliness. He lived by Rubashov's code: 'Honour is to be useful without vanity.'[7] He naturally compared himself with the martyr-heroes of his day: Prynne, Burton and Bastwick, who seemed to symbolise, by their suffering, the romantic defiance which he deprecated. But even *their* position as martyrs was misleading. All three said that they were moderate Anglicans. Yet even in 1637 Burton was a congregationalist, and owned up in 1644 about his motives in carrying out the deception: 'the more cautelous and self-wise, or discreet any of us (but especially my self) then was, to avoid the fear of men, or force of law'.[8] His fellow-sufferer, John Bastwick, poured scorn on the 'new light' doctrines of Independency that allowed Burton so much scope:

> That if that which seemeth a truth to them today, do tomorrow appear otherwise by some new light . . . and they be convinced by that light that they were in an error before, they are to relinquish their former tenant, whatsoever it were, and to follow that new light that God hath appeared to them in.

But his hands were no cleaner than Burton's. It is clear that even in 1637 he was no moderate Anglican but a convinced Presbyterian. And what but the idea of 'progressive comprehension' lay behind his boast about 'my glory and honour, upon better information and more mature deliberation and judgment to have renounced all those errors, and to have embraced the truth', when speaking of his distance now from an earlier sympathy with the views of Lilburne?[9] Prynne alone meant what he said at the scaffold; he alone had no time for cant or equivocation. One reason that he hated plays was that acting required men 'to seeme that in outward which they are not in truthe'. He attacked dissemblers on and off the stage: Burton; John Durie ('his conscience tender, yet stretching and mutable with times and preferments'); Hugh Peter ('If Master Peter be now of another

Judgement, it manifests either his grosse ignorance or temporizing then, or his levity now'); John Goodwin ('his conscience wheeling from one side and opinion to another so often').[10]

It is important not to sentimentalise Prynne's position. From a distrust of power, which is almost holy, figures of our own time, like George Orwell and Simone Weil, become 'refugees from the camp of victory'.[11] Orwell, in a famous essay, once quoted the Revivalist hymn:

> Dare to be a Daniel,
> Dare to stand alone;
> Dare to have a purpose firm,
> Dare to make it known.

Orwell suggested that the hymn could be brought up to date simply by adding 'Don't' at the beginning of each line.[12] He referred back with longing to the Protestant cult of the heretic: of the man who refused to outrage his conscience. Prynne would seem to be cast in that heroic mould. It was an opponent who said of him:

> I am confident that whatsoever Mr. P. writeth (though I approve not all that is set out in his name) he writeth with a very upright and sincere heart.[13]

But Prynne had no distrust of power or abstract love of freedom. His pamphlet, *The Sword of Christian Magistracy*, is one of the most blood-curdling pleas for total repressive action from the civil authority in the English language. And, in the period between 1641 and 1645 when he was a follower of Brightman and 'root and branch', he kept remarkably quiet about the dangers of a Presbyterian theocracy. Henry Robinson pointed out how implausible it was to suppose that suddenly, in 1645, Prynne should discover such dangers.[14] The truth was that Prynne was willing to entrust total power in the hands of the civil magistrate (after 1645), or of the London 'root and branch' clergy (before 1645), *provided that a real reformation of morals was effected*. Henry Burton pointed out to Prynne the unrealistic nature of his hopes in 1644: England 'cannot become a Mount Sion in one day'.[15] But that was precisely what the London 'root and branch' ministers had led him to expect, and Prynne was unconvinced by party-line excuses, whether from an Independent like Burton or from a Presbyterian like Gillespie.

If Godly Prince or Godly People or Godly Parliament had really effected a speedy reformation of morals, Prynne would have seemed no Orwellian figure. But they didn't, and so he did. His opponents argued that Prynne's empiricism betrayed a lack of sophistication: he ought not to be so concerned with such superficialities as external conduct. There is something in this argument. Bunyan referred once to a colleague: 'I found him although a good man, a stranger to much combat with the Devil.'[16] This combat is lacking in Prynne: he is the least auto-biographical of writers. There is a chilling lack of introspection which makes this most Puritan pamphleteer seem least Puritan; which makes him more truly a figure of the second half of the seventeenth century than of the first half. Prynne, distrustful of ultimate ends, concentrating on immediate means, was not capable of the moral gymnastics that his contemporaries performed.

Moral gymnastics came easily to men who were more worried about enforcing virtue than about attaining it; whose concern was to create a moral code, not to abide by one. These men, working for a Godly Rule, would argue that an omelette cannot be made without breaking eggs: Prynne's scruples about the eggs – about, for instance, the parish that was denied the pastoral care of Mr Tanner simply because he had been a malignant – would seem to them ludicrously misplaced. Honour to them was not decency, as the tsarist prisoner in the cell next to Rubashov had naïvely supposed it to be. Rather, as Rubashov asserted, it was to be useful without vanity. Decency concerned the sanctity of means; usefulness concerned the relevance to ends. Between 1603 and 1660 the great arguments over religion tend to be fought less over the propriety of individual actions than upon their relevance to furthering the ends of 'Godly Rule'. But arguments over means slide imperceptibly into arguments over ends:

> Show us not the aim without the way
> For ends and means on earth are so entangled
> That changing one, you change the other too.
> Each different path brings other ends in view.[17]

English Protestants followed different paths to their common goal of a 'Godly Rule', between 1603 and 1660, but found at the Restoration that other ends *had* been brought to view. The great truisms of the first half of the seventeenth century – the unity of Jerusalem, the need for a coerced virtue, the imminence of the end of the world and of the destruction of Antichrist – no longer rang true.

One of the reasons that the pursuits of *ends* had become suspect was that they had become associated with the millenarian fantasies of cranks. Mr Christopher Hill has a charming essay on one such crank, John Mason. Mason had a very revealing conversation with a Mr Ives in the 1690s. When Mason protested that he was sure that 'Christ is now entering upon his Reign here, as really as ever King Charles, King James or King William Reign'd', Mr Ives advised him to 'let Blood speedily'. Mr Hill points out how different was this rationalist reaction of the 1690s to such ideas, when compared with earlier years. But the antithesis that he draws is not quite exact: 'For over a century millenarianism had been a socially terrifying doctrine, associated with violent revolution.'[18] It had been that, but it had been more than that. The purpose of this brief study of religious controversies has been to show some of the ways in which millenarian thinking coloured the presumptions of the socially *acceptable* as well: of James I's views of kingship and those of his loyal Nonconformist subjects; of the Laudians' ideas of clerical rule; of the 'root and branch' ministers' enthusiasm for a Covenant and for an Assembly of Divines; of the Erastians' criticisms of 1645; and even – at least on the Independents' side – their efforts at union with Presbyterian ministers in the Commonwealth. Mountague in 1625 had deplored the confidence with which men accepted, from a reading of the Book of Revelation, that Rome was Antichrist: 'it is a Prophecy; and therefore a Mystery sealed up, obscure, not manifested, not to bee understood, but by evident and plaine event, without divine revelation'.[19] He was, at that time, not contending with cranks but with a widely held assumption. Yet when Mr Mason offers to unseal this Mystery he is advised to 'let Blood speedily'. The Millennium, once the cure, had become a symptom. The defiant words of 1625 had become platitudes in the period after the Restoration. Men were all Mountagues now. That was the revolution.

Yet we must be clear about the nature of this revolution. It was a revulsion from the idea of a 'Godly Rule', not from the idea of godly behaviour. In the do-gooding activities of the Latitudinarians we have observed a reversal of the priorities of Gosse's father: conduct, not faith, was what mattered now. The immorality associated with the Restoration Court gives a certain plausibility to the idea that the abandonment of the search for a 'Godly Rule' was bound up with the abandonment of moral standards. This is not true: by the time of the Restoration the sects, like the Ranters, that continue the search for a 'Godly Rule' are also identified with antinomianism; while men such as Pepys and Clarendon, who had never been touched by the vision of a 'Godly Rule', could feel most keenly the moral lapses of Court life.[20] Clarendon's Tew Circle of the 1630s, with its chaste, rationalist, anti-clerical leanings, its antipathy to 'that sea of wine, and women, and quarrels, and gaming', its great emphasis on the value of personal relationships and integrity, was even then much closer in spirit to the Latitudinarians and Cambridge Platonists after the Restoration than to their more flexible contemporaries who were searching for a 'Godly Rule'. Clarendon knew that the ends never did justify the means:

> Whereas the true logic is, that the thing desired is not necessary, if the ways are unlawful, which are proposed to bring it to pass.[21]

During the Civil War Colonel Fiennes had to defend his decision to surrender Bristol to the Royalists instead of burning it down. He took his stand upon 'not doing evill that good might come of it, a diviner Law having a greater influence on his soule at that time, than the Law of War'. Prynne, writing in the heat of battle, called this excuse 'an unparalleled affront against Law and publike justice, which patience it self cannot endure'.[22] But we have seen that Prynne himself was a somewhat isolated figure in his time in his preoccupation with *means* rather than *ends,* and after the Restoration his admiration for the *gravitas* and integrity of

Clarendon, the man who respected the sanctity of *means*, was unfeigned, unreserved, though also, alas, unreciprocated.[23]

How are we to explain the primacy of means over ends after the Restoration? Why had the ideal of a 'Godly Rule' lost its power to arouse men? Can we explain it simply in terms of the decline of Calvinism, the growth of cynicism, or the rise of toleration? There is something in each of these explanations. Yet none of these, in itself, is a *total* explanation.

The ideal of a 'Godly Rule' was shattered as much by the *resurgence* of Calvinist feeling as by its *decline*. This seems paradoxical until we remember that John Foxe had offered a heterodox comfort, which Calvin himself would have repudiated. Foxe had shown generations of English Protestants that their Marian predecessors had made no worthless sacrifice. He had shown them that the burning of the martyrs fell into place in the general pattern of God's Design. When we discuss Calvinists' resistance theories or attitude to bishops we properly make a distinction between *Calvin* and *Calvinists*: that what holds true of Calvin's followers, like Beza and Knox, is not necessarily true of Calvin himself. We do not make equal allowance for the gap between Calvin and his followers in their millenarian views. Calvin showed less interest than almost all his followers in eschatology. Like St Augustine, he viewed the Apocalypse with detachment: the Book of Revelation had a circumscribed, allegorical significance, and that was all. Henry More ruefully surveyed Calvin's few indecisive probes into the Apocalypse and then declared roundly that, in this respect at least, Calvin was no Calvinist![24] At the core of Foxe's work, on the other hand, was a blasphemy: the claim to be privy to the Secrets of Calvin's Inscrutable God. Here indeed was the *rationale* for a 'Godly Rule': the attempt to fashion a way of life that would be pleasing to Him. The critics of Foxe attacked details in his claim, but left untouched the central blasphemy that underlay it. The Laudians gleefully showed that Foxe had got it wrong: God favoured bishops, not princes. They did not (with the exception of Mountague) see anything wrong in the attempt to read God's Mind. The same was true of Foxe's Puritan critics. The Book of Revelation held the key to God's Design?

Yes, but one no longer needed a prince or martyr-bishop to unlock it.

They disputed Foxe's answers, not his questions. To dispute his *questions* – to believe that any attempt to find in Scripture the pattern of rule pleasing to God was doomed to failure – required a different approach. That approach is part of the general secularisation of politics and history which lies outside the scope of this present small study and has, in any case, been given close attention in several valuable recent works.[25] But not enough comparable attention has been paid to the part that Calvinists themselves played in this development. Not Calvin's *immediate* followers; though, arguably, his more *attentive* followers. One critic, Mr L. V. Bredvold, has remarked: 'The influence of Augustine sometimes parallels or interweaves with the influence of Montaigne or Sextus Empiricus.'[26] We are aware enough of the blows to the notion of a 'Godly Rule' that were struck by sceptics like Hobbes and Selden. We are less aware of the extent to which, in the late 1640s and throughout the 1650s, many Calvinists could join the cynics in disparaging the efforts of men to fashion a 'Godly Rule' simply by reverting to the old Augustinian truths that had once satisfied Calvin himself. As Mr Bredvold reminds us, 'the Augustinian doctrine of grace, according to which the intellectual as well as the moral faculties of men are in their present fallen state totally useless towards salvation, had both in Augustine and among his followers an effect parallel to philosophical scepticism'.[27] In the seventeenth century it meant that Thomas Browne could be a sceptic *and* a Calvinist; Pascal, a disciple of Montaigne *and* a Jansenist. The American historian, Perry Miller, once made a perceptive comparison between Pascal and Roger Williams.[28] It is a useful reminder to us that the stand of men such as Pascal, Browne and Williams against the textual literalism which set up repressive 'Godly Rules' on earth could come, not from *disowning* Calvinism but from *affirming* it. This meant that Roger Williams, champion of religious toleration, could feel no affinity with the Quakers, champions of religious toleration. Williams, a rigid Calvinist, argued that 'of the essence of being of the immortal, invisible, infinite, eternal, omnipotent and omniscient, and wise, we know no more than a fly knows what a king is'. But the Quakers did claim to know more: this presumption wounded Williams. So he could think no better of 'this proud Fox' because they shared an antipathy to clerical discipline; doctrinal heterodoxy was to the Calvinist a terrible, almost intolerable, price to pay for religious freedom. Inasmuch as 'Godly Rule' – the claim indeed to know more about God's Plan than a fly knows about a king – was a *pseudo-Calvinist* ideal it could be rejected by *anti-Calvinists*, such as George Fox and his Quakers, but also by *true Calvinists*, such as Williams, Coleman, Prynne, Cromwell and Erastus himself.

If the destruction of 'Godly Rule' cannot simply be identified with the decline of Calvinism, neither can it simply be identified with the rise of cynicism. Selden, Cotton, Hobbes: these men had a real part to play in the war on clerical pretensions. But Cromwell would not have called his rule 'Godless'; if we have argued that this is the *effect* of his actions, we have not argued that this is their *motive*. We have noted the *idealism* that led men such as Cromwell, Coleman and Williams – by very different routes – to reject the idea of an imposed godly pattern on earth.

But if it was not cynicism that linked Cromwell with Selden in a rejection of 'Godly Rule' any more than it was doctrine that linked Fox and Williams in a similar stand, at least all four shared the ideal of religious toleration. Is this the common denominator? Assume this, and one has to omit from our story Erastus, Coleman, Prynne and their colleagues. The Erastian revival in the late 1640s was *not* a plea for religious toleration. Since its adversary was an intolerant Assembly of Divines, this was how it could seem to contemporaries. But Coleman, Prynne and their colleagues were Calvinists who believed that the reprobate majority *must* be disciplined into virtue (they were outraged by 'toleratorists'); they no longer believed, however, that the clerics *were* the men to administer that discipline.

Is there a common denominator? Our last two chapters looked very closely at what at first sight might seem a minor ecclesiastical dispute: the controversy over the admission of men to the Sacrament of the Lord's Supper. One pamphleteer called it 'the great bone of contention in the Church of God this day'.[29] This is not surprising because the issues that it raised were crucial. They were the issues that Erastus had first raised against Wither at Heidelberg. They were the issues that Calvin, in his teasingly opaque way, had left obscured. Michael Walzer has brought out well Calvin's dilemma:

> Because of Calvin's exalted view of God's sovereignty, he could not claim that the Church's excommunication was an absolute condemnation to an eternity in hell; on the other hand, he dared not surrender such a powerful disciplinary instrument.[30]

If the controversy had been the simple lay backlash to overweening clerical claims – which is how some of the laymen, some of the clerics, were anxious to portray it – it could never have aroused the passions that it did. It tore at the heart of English Protestantism because it mirrored its confusions. Men 'who dared not surrender such a powerful disciplinary instrument' believed that they were the heirs of Calvin. Men who held 'an exalted view of God's sovereignty' believed that they were the heirs of Calvin. Both were right. It was typical of the confused nature of the controversy that *both* sides appealed to the old traditions of English Nonconformity. Thus when the Independent ministers drew up their Declaration at the Savoy Conference on 12 October 1658 they claimed that it was in 'full concurrence' with 'the old Puritan Nonconformists, Foxe, Dering, Greenham, Cartwright, Fenner, Fulke, Whittaker, Reynolds, Perkins, etc.'. And they argued (Chapter 30, article 8) for an unmixed communion.[31] Similarly, the Independent Anthony Palmer had based hopes for a reunion with Presbyterianism on a common acceptance of the need to preserve the purity of communion: he had seen this aspiration as rooted in older English traditions of Nonconformity.[32] Collings also argued that the burden upon the consciences of the old Nonconformists had not been the barriers erected against free admission to the Lord's Table but the absence of such barriers. Thus it was the advocates of free admission who were turning their backs on the traditions of old Nonconformity.[33]

The fact that Collings had to argue this point shows the power of the opposing case: that the heirs of old Nonconformity *were* those who opposed rigid barriers of admission. One of the most influential of these advocates was John Timson. He claimed that the victory of his point of view in the controversy – 'of greater concernment than most even of these that are godly have or do judge it to be' – would bring together Presbyterian and Independent, 'especially the orthodox party of both'. It is a reflection upon the confusing cross-currents of the time that Timson's claim was not disingenuous. He reasoned that approval of free admission to the Sacraments could unite those who held the 'church-ideal', whether Presbyterians or Independents: in other words, those who accepted the need for a National Church to discipline the ungodly. And remember that Timson, like Prynne and Coleman, appealed for admission to the Sacraments as a *disciplinary* measure, not as the *renunciation of discipline*. Anthony Palmer, on the other hand, had argued that approval of suspending powers could unite those who held the 'sect-ideal', whether Presbyterians or Independents: in other words, those who accepted the need for the pure to separate themselves from the company of the ungodly. One of the weaknesses in Prynne's pamphleteering against the Independents was that he never – like Timson – made a serious attempt to distinguish the Independency of a Henry Burton from that of a Philip Nye.[34] But Timson and Prynne agreed on one thing: that free admission was no novel tenet but the regular practice among old Nonconformists: 'And will any say that our first reformers were not godly and learned men?' Timson defined reformation in the Church as the bringing of people into outward conformity with Christ's Laws. The extent of his craving for a National Church was evident in his nostalgia for Elizabeth I:

> And the memory of Queen Elizabeth in this Nation is blessed, because of her care to restrain the Papists from their superstition and cruelty, and to draw on the whole people of the Nation to the Protestant Religion.[35]

In a letter to Baxter, John Humfrey stressed the value of Timson's contribution. Humfrey described Timson as 'a man that follows the plow all day and studyes and then writes down his thoughtes and reades at night'. Humfrey stressed Timson's links with Jacobean Nonconformity: that he had been a pupil of Robert Bolton.[36] One Presbyterian, Roger Drake, called Humfrey's own advocacy of free admission 'meer Church-Levelling'.[37] Mr Christopher Hill has noted that the emphasis of Presbyterians in opposition tended to be on spiritual equality, 'with appropriate vagueness about the precise individuals who were equal'.[38] As Calvinists, Prynne and Humfrey were no 'Church-levellers', no egalitarians; they believed, as firmly as did Drake and Collings, in the existence of the Elect. But as Calvinists, with a belief in the Omnipotence and Inscrutability of God, they resented the attempt, implicit in the more rigorous rules for admission to the Sacrament, to clarify that 'appropriate vagueness' about the Elect. Thus they could delusively be represented as champions of human equality, and be joined in their fight on this issue by men who *were* just that. And this underlines once more the importance of the issue of the clerical suspending powers[39]: it could bring together in opposition to such claims men who cared about equality and men who did not, men who cared about toleration and men who did not, men who cared about the powers of the civil magistrate and men who did not, men who were idealists and men who were cynical, men who were anti-Calvinistic and men who were rigidly Calvinistic.

The appeals that both sides in the controversy made to 'old nonconformity' were sincere but misplaced. Men could invoke the memory of Foxe, Jewel and Reynolds and the Elizabethan Church, but they could not recapture the millenarian energy that gave point to that tradition. Timson, following the plough all day and studying at night, might have been a pupil of Robert Bolton, but he could not recapture in the 1650s Bolton's terrible vision in 1621 of a society without a Godly Prince: 'Murder, adulteries, incests, rapes, roberies, perjuries, witchcrafts, blasphemies, all kinds of villanies, outrages, and savage cruelty, would overflow all Countries.'[40]

Bolton believed that this would happen once you took 'Soveraignty from the face of the earth'. But he was writing at a time when it was possible to believe that sovereignty would not be taken from the earth: this was the point of his fulsome tributes to Foxe's second Constantine, Queen Elizabeth. He was still echoing Calvinistic pessimism about the nature of Man. So too the London 'root and branch' minister, Thomas Wilson, promised the Commons in 1641 that 'vile persons that spake villany' would have their mouths stopped. He was promising a moral reformation, in other words, without sacrificing a Calvinist conviction in the vileness of vile persons. This was the beauty of the Apocalypse: God would bring about reformation, not Man. But when the Apocalypse became, during the Civil War, more and more associated with the lunatic fringe and therefore suspect, what was to become of that moral reformation? John Goodwin was one minister who had been touched in the early 1640s, like Wilson and Bolton, by a millenarian expectation of moral reform. He had, at that stage, looked to the imminent downfall of Antichrist and to 'executing the judgments of God upon the Whore'. By 1646 he was *implicitly* attacking chiliasm in his warning about 'unpolitic Christians' who 'catch at the spiritual privileges of New Jerusalem before it comes down from heaven'. By 1653 this was transformed (as with Cromwell), into an *explicit* attack on Fifth Monarchy Men and Ranters. This did not mean that Goodwin lost faith in a reform of morals. Villainous mouths *would* be stopped. But how? By a personal regeneration: vile persons were no longer vile. In his pamphlet, *The Pagans Debt and Dowry*, of 1651, Goodwin attacked the view that men were irredeemably vile. The price he then paid for going on believing in the possibilities of ethical reform was doctrinal heterodoxy. 'Godly Rule' had become godly behaviour. And what of those who remained Calvinists? The concept of a 'Godly Rule' came to seem blasphemous to those very Calvinists who had hungered for it.

The discovery of the blasphemy was a slow and painful process of disenchantment. First, men had to rid themselves of the illusion that God favoured Princes; then bishops; then presbyters; then Parliament; then Army. Then – and only then – when the successive illusions had been peeled off could Calvinists be recalled to the austerities of their founder's creed: that the God whom they worshipped was Unknowable. They too would have to settle for means, not ends; for the private action rather than the public discipline (without even Goodwin's faith in the *merits* of the private action). At the end of the Civil War William Prynne – once the zealous interpreter of God's Will – perfectly captured the tired mood of such men:

> For my part, I have seen so much experience in the world, that I dare trust none with my own or the Kingdoms safety but God alone . . . we have seen such strange Mutabilities and perfidiousnesse in men of all sorts since our troubles that we cannot trust neither the King nor Prince, City nor Countrey, this Generall nor that Generall; this Army, nor those that went before it, and yet our selves who are jealous one of another, treacherous one to another, distrustful of all.[41]

The Calvinist discovers Original Sin and registers his disapproval! This was not the mood of a man setting out to establish a 'Godly Rule': it reveals how amputated Calvinism became when it lost its millenarian confidence, and when the Apocalypse was taken over by the political and social extremists of the mid-seventeenth century (the Ranters and Fifth Monarchy Men), and by the psychotics and neurotics of later times (men like John Mason and Edmund Gosse's father).

It is quite true that the millenarian ideas of Ranters and Fifth Monarchy Men have a boldness and clarity which is absent from earlier speculations. But that is the mark of their weakness, not of their strength. If the followers of Foxe and Brightman were vague about the day of the Last Judgement this was a conscious act of policy on their part. The New England Minister, Urian Oakes, brought out well the sophisticated intelligence which he and his colleagues needed to bring to scriptural interpretation:

> 'Sapience or Wisdome properly belongs to Syllogistical Judgement, and is a virtue of the Understanding whereby a man discerns the dependance of things, and how one follows upon another. [It] imports in it a laying of things together in a Syllogistical way. Hence when men reason amiss and conclude that which is not virtually contained in the Premises, or make wrong inferences, they, are said to Paralogise themselves. . . .[42]

By the late 1640s men were no longer so ready to defer to the 'Sapience' or 'Wisdome' of the learned clergy: the Erastian controversy, in particular, destroyed their prestige. They were swept aside by the new men – less erudite, less cautious, more literal than their predecessors – who soon had 'Paralogised themselves' into Fifth Monarchy beliefs. Millenarianism was then truly – what it had never been before – a creed for cranks.

1. Edmund Gosse, *Father and Son* (Four Square Books, 1959) p. 182. Gosse follows this point up with an illustration: 'We may search the famous "Rule and Exercises of Holy Living" from cover to cover, and not learn that Jeremy Taylor would have thought that any activity of the district-visitor or the Salvation lassie came within the category of saintliness.' Taylor is perhaps not the happiest example: the woman of noble birth, for instance, *was* counselled in the *Rule and Exercises of Holy Living* not only to 'read good books, pray often and speak little' but also to 'visit poor cottages, and relieve their necessity'. Nevertheless Gosse's general point is a good one and has relevance for Taylor (even if Gosse overstated it). Taylor's preoccupation with *ends* in the same work is well reflected in the statement, 'Holy intention is to the actions of a man that which the soul is to the body'; the care with which Taylor develops rules for assessing purity of intentions; his approving quotation of *Seneca's maxim*: 'The same things are honest and dishonest: the manner of doing them, and the end of the designe, makes the separation.' Finally, Taylor says of God's Grace that 'it sanctifies the most common action of our life; and yet so necessary that, without it, the very best actions of our devotion are imperfect and vicious' (*English Prose 1600–1660*, ed. V. Harris and I. Husain (New York, 1965) pp. 473–88).

2. Kenyon, *The Stuart Constitution*, p. 358.

3. Baxter would have resisted the comparison, yet his own changing views on the relative importance of faith and conduct reflect – in a subdued way – the same tendency. Baxter, *Autobiography*, pp. 112–13, acknowledged that in his younger days he had been irked by talk of God being good and Heaven blessed: 'I had rather know how I may attain it.' But the older Baxter found that regeneration and the marks of sincerity were no longer his major preoccupation.

4. John Tickell, *The Bottomless Pit Smoaking* ... (London, 1651) pp. 37–40.

5. Woodhouse, *Puritanism and Liberty*, p. 45. This was what Samuel Butler (*Hudibras*, ii, II 133, 137) found odious in the Puritan saint:

> For breaking of an oath and lying
> Is but a kind of self-denying
> A saint-like virtue, and from hence
> Some have broke oaths by Providence.

6. *Calendar State Papers Domestic, Charles I, 1637–1638*, p. 296.

7. Thomas Sheppard put the New England case against martyrdom: 'And whom the Lord will honour by suffering for his Cause, by imprisonment, etc., he gives them spirits suitable thereto: whom the Lord will reserve for other service, or imploy in other places, he inclines their breasts rather to fly, giving them an breast suitable to such a condition': *The Puritans*, ed. P. Miller and T. Johnson, I 119.

8. Henry Burton, *A Vindication* ..., p. 72.

9. John Bastwick, *The Second Part of that Booke* ... (London, 1645) p. 35.

10. Prynne: *A Full Reply* ... (London, 1644) p. 7; *The Time-Serving Proteus and Ambidexter Divine* ... (London, 1650) p. 2; *A Fresh Discovery* ... (London, 1645) p. 33; *The Sword of Christian Magistracy* ... (London, 1653) p. 162.

11. Richard Rees, *Fugitive from the Camp of Victory* (London, 1961).

12. George Orwell, 'The Prevention of Literature', in *Selected Essays* (Penguin, 1960) p. 160.

13. John Ley, *The New Querie* (London, 1695) p. 46. This is a most impressive tribute since, as we have seen, by 1645 the gap between Prynne and Presbyterians like Ley is wide, and was being exploited at the time by Ley's Independent opponent, John Saltmarsh.

14. Henry Robinson, *The Falsehood of Mr William Pryn's Truth Triumphing* ... (London, 1645) p. 7.

15. Henry Burton, *A Vindication of Churches Commonly called Independent* (London, 1644) p. 1.

16. John Bunyan, *Grace Abounding*, ed. J. Brown (London, 1707) p. 55.

17. Ferdinand Lassalle, *Franz von Sickingen*: quoted in Arthur Koestler, *Darkness at Noon* (Penguin Modern Classics, 1964) p. 19.

18. Christopher Hill, 'John Mason and the End of the World', in *Puritanism and Revolution,* pp. 334–5.

19. Richard Mountague, *Appello Caesarem* (London, 1625) p. 146.

20. Pepys commented on 4 September 1668 that while he enjoyed the wit of Ben Jonson, 'the business of abusing the Puritans begins to grow stale, and of no use, they being the people that at last will be found the wisest'. Cf. Clarendon's moving tribute to Falkland's ethical stature: *Selections,* p. 67.

21. Clarendon, *Selections,* pp. 21, 22, 205. Clarendon was obsessed with ends and means. Cromwell to him personified the cant of the Puritan saint: 'the greatest dissembler living' (pp. 305–6). He thought that the only difference between Presbyterians and Independents was that the Presbyterians were not quite Machiavellian enough: they retained the odd scruple (p. 309). Richard Baxter (*Autobiography,* p. 88) also saw Cromwell in this light: 'He thinketh that the end being good and necessary, the necessary means cannot be bad.' But he was able to correct Clarendon on one point. Clarendon thought that Cromwell, the arch-dissembler, had even played the Presbyterian: 'He sung all psalms with them to their tunes, and loved the longest sermons as much as they' (Clarendon, *Selections,* p. 306). But Baxter (*Autobiography,* p. 89) pointed out that 'he never endeavoured to persuade the Presbyterians that he was one of them', and indeed Baxter, in his tribute to the Committee of Triers and to the freedom that he enjoyed in the Protectorate which we have already noted, was obliquely recognising Cromwell's developing scruples about means.

22. William Prynne and Clement Walker, *A True and Full Relation* . . . (London, 1643) dedicatory epistle.

23. Prynne dedicated one of his works of 1664 (*The Fourth Part of a Brief Register* . . .) to Clarendon as 'a visible expression of my real gratitude, for the many Noble Favours, Civilities I have received upon all occasions from your Lordship'. He referred to the encouragement which he had received from Clarendon to write a history of the struggle between Papal ambitions and Parliament's resolutions. He had not completed it then (this was his *An Exact Chronological History, 1666–1670,* and offered this work as a substitute. He was convinced that Clarendon's impeachment was a Popish Plot. Clarendon, on the other hand, thought little of Prynne (*History of the Rebellion,* I 265–6), and indeed Prynne's works were high among the 'ill books' from which he derived a masochistic pleasure in exile (*Calendar of the Clarendon State Papers,* I 372).

24. Tuveson, *Millennium and Utopia*, p. 222.

25. Among them: J. G. A. Pocock, *The Ancient Constitution and the Feudal Law* (Cambridge University Press, 1957); W. H. Greenleaf, *Order, Empiricism and Politics* (Oxford University Press, 1964); Felix Raab, *The English Face of Machiavelli* (London, Routledge, 1964); and Pocock's interesting *critique* of Raab: ' "The Only Politician": Machiavelli, Harrington and Felix Raab', *Historical Studies: Australia and New Zealand*, 12, no. 46 pp. 265–96.

26. L. V. Bredvold, *The Intellectual Milieu of John Dryden* (Ann Arbor Paperbacks, p. 92). Jasper Mayne, *The Peoples War* ... (London, 1647), makes superb use of Sextus Empiricus in an attack on 'an army of Mussell-men' for seeking to coerce men into virtue. The whole pamphlet is a witty, under-rated anticipation of Locke.

27. Bredvold, *Intellectual Milieu* ..., p. 24.

28. Perry Miller, 'Roger Williams, His Contribution to the American Tradition', *Roger Williams and the Massachusetts Magistrates*, ed. T. P. Green (Boston, Heath, 1964) p. 111.

29. John Collings, *Responsoria Bipartita* ... (London, 1655) no pagination.

30. Walzer, *Revolution of the Saints*, p. 53.

31. Benjamin Hanbury, *Historical Memorials* (London, 1844) III 531, 544.

32. Anthony Palmer, *A Scripture-Rule*, pp. 3, 5, 7.

33. Collings, *Responsoria Bipartita*, no pagination.

34. A non-separating congregationalist like Nye could find Burton's belittling references to a National Church offensive: 'shall I tell Mr Burton what Mr Nye said again and again of his *Protestation Protested.* I will if he will not be angry with him, it was this, that in that Book there was grosse Brownisme which he nor his Brethren no way agreed with him in and that for his part he would as soon subscribe to the Book of Common Prayer, as to divers things there ...' (Thomas Edwards, *Gangraena* ..., III 243). Edwards, a notorious Presbyterian muck-raker, is an unreliable source, and yet what we know of Nye's principles (Nobbs, see above, p. 160) makes his story quite likely. It is knowledge of such cleavages that makes A. S. P. Woodhouse (*Puritanism and Liberty*, p. 36) reluctant to identify Independency simply with the 'sect-ideal'. But the situation that we have traced is even more complex: of Presbyterians attracted to the 'sect-ideal' as much as Independents to the 'church-ideal'. There is a very intelligent analysis by a contemporary, *Sirrahnio* (i.e. John Harris), *The Royal Quarrel* (London, 1647), who recognises that

the real division is not between Presbyterians and Independents, but between 'Reall Presbyterians' and 'Reall Independents' (for whom Collings was speaking) on the one hand and, on the other, 'Royall Presbyterians' and 'Royal Independents' (for whom Timson was speaking).

35. John Timson, *The Bar to Free Admission To the Lords Supper Removed* ... (London, 1654) dedicatory epistle, pp. 85, 153, 155, 193.

36. (Doctor Williams's Library) Baxter MSS. 59.1, f. 193.

37. Roger Drake, *A Boundary to the Holy Mount* ... (London, 1653) preface.

38. Christopher Hill, *Oliver Cromwell, 1658–1958* (Historical Association Pamphlet, 1958) p. 10.

39. The confusions provoked by this issue can be illustrated by the differing attitudes taken by the Puritan martyrs, Prynne, Burton and Bastwick. Prynne saw toleration and suspension as twin vices, which sprang from a common indifference to the need to discipline the ungodly; Burton saw toleration and suspension as twin virtues, which sprang from a common concern for the purity of congregations; Bastwick saw suspension as a virtue which destroyed the argument for toleration, which he regarded as a vice.

40. Robert Bolton, *Two Sermons* (London, 1635) p. 21.

41. William Prynne, *The Substance of a Speech* ... (London, 1641) p. 76.

42. Quoted in *The Puritans*, ed. P. Miller and T. Johnson ..., I, 25.

Select Bibliography

This is a guide to some of the works which have been useful in this study.

1. PRIMARY: UNPRINTED

A. *Bodleian Library, Oxford*. Cherry MSS. 2: some useful side-light on the activities of Archbishop Laud's greatest enemy within the church, John Williams.

B. *British Museum*. Stowe MSS. 180, 182, 184, 743, 744: the private correspondence of Sir Edward Dering is a useful corrective to his own public account of his activities.

C. *Doctor Williams's Library*. Baxter MSS. 59: the casuist gifts of Richard Baxter are displayed to advantage in this voluminous, under-used correspondence.

D. *House of Lords Record Office*. Braye MSS.: *Proceedings Against Strafford and Laud*: the record (from a Puritan source) of Archbishop Laud's trial which goes a long way towards undermining the official Puritan version produced by William Prynne.

2. PRIMARY: PRINTED

The basis of this study was the huge pamphlet literature in the Thomason Collection in the British Museum. There are full lists in: A. W. POLLARD and C. R. REDGRAVE, *Short-title Catalogue of Books . . . 1475–1640* (London, 1926); D. WING, *Short-title Catalogue of Books . . . 1641–1700* (New York, 1945).

ROBERT BAILLIE, *Letters and Journals . . .*, ed. D. Laing (Edinburgh, 1841–2). How the religious struggles of the 1640s appeared to a partisan Scottish observer. He is seriously under-rated by historians like W. A. Shaw (see below).

RICHARD BAXTER, *Autobiography* (London, Everyman's Library, 1931). The classic Puritan autobiography: strongest of all in its evocation of what it was like to be a young English Puritan in the early seventeenth century.

THOMAS CARLYLE, ed., *Oliver Cromwell's Letters and Speeches* ... (London, Ward & Lock, 1897), is now superseded by W. C. Abbott's more scholarly edition (Cambridge, Mass., 1937–47). I am delighted to see from a shy bibliographical note by M. Walzer (see below) that he shares my truant preference for the exuberant breathlessness of a Carlyle.

CLARENDON, *Selections*, ed. G. Huehns (Oxford University Press, 1953): particularly interesting to compare with Baxter's views of English morality before the Civil War.

SIMONDS D'EWES, *Autobiography and Correspondence* ..., ed. J. O. Halliwell (London, Bentley, 1845). The Puritan aspirations of a seemingly staid dry-as-dust come across with moving force.

JOHN FOXE, *The Acts and Monuments* ..., ed. S. R. Cattley (London, 1836–41). A decisive influence on generations of English Protestants and perhaps the key factor in explaining why English Puritanism was more complex than a 'revolution of the saints'.

PETER HEYLYN, *Cyprianus Anglicus* ... (London, 1668). If Laud had been less reticent, this loving biography would have been less important. As it is, it constitutes an unique insight into the aspirations of the Laudians.

THOMAS HOBBES, *Leviathan* (London, Everyman's Library): the most subtle statement of what is usually (and falsely) described as the Erastian ideal.

JOHN JEWEL, *Works* (Cambridge, 1849): complements Foxe's defence of the sixteenth-century Church.

WILLIAM LAUD, *Works* (London, 1823–4): in the absence of a definitive *apologia*, this is the next best thing. Occasionally we are given teasing insights into his philosophy by an odd comment or even an odd dream: my Sussex colleague, Mr U. P. Burke, is at present engaged in the heroic task of trying to derive a psycho-analytical interpretation of the Archbishop from the thirty dreams which he recorded in his journal.

JOHN LIGHTFOOT, *Works* (London, 1823–4): a lesser man than Hobbes, of course, but arguably more representative of the Erastian opposition to the Westminster Assembly which flowered in the late 1640s.

Minutes of the Sessions of the Westminster Assembly of Divines ..., eds. A. Mitchell and J. Stuthers (Edinburgh, 1874): valuable as a formal record of the Erastian controversy. Needs to be supplemented by close investigation of the pamphlets of the time for the full implication of these debates to emerge.

JOHN SELDEN, *Table Talk*, ed. F. Pollock (London, Quaritch, 1927): memorable epigrammatic thrusts at the clerics.

SURTEES SOCIETY, LII, *The Correspondence of John Cosin*, ed. G. Ornsby: shows what Selden was up against. This correspondence of a leading Laudian brings out the claustrophobic intimacy of one wing of the Church in the 1630s, which could see even the blameless Joseph Hall as a Puritan.

Among the more useful of the collections of source materials are: WILLIAM HALLER, *Tracts on Liberty in the Puritan Revolution 1638–47* (New York, 1965); WILLIAM HALLER and GODFREY DAVIES, *The Leveller Tracts* (New York, 1944); P. MILLER and T. JOHNSON, *The Puritans* (Harper Torchbooks, 1965); D. M. WOLFE, *Leveller Manifestos of the Puritan Revolution* (New York, 1944); A. S. P. WOODHOUSE, *Puritanism and Liberty* (London, Dent, 1950): valuable not only as a record of the Putney and Whitehall Debates, but also for its dazzling introductory essay on the nature of seventeenth-century Puritanism.

J. P. KENYON, *The Stuart Constitution* (Cambridge University Press, 1966), differs from all the preceding collections in that it attempts to sum up a century, not a movement within the century. It is the most comprehensive paperback collection of seventeenth-century documents that we have. The choice of contemporary material is often flat and uninspired but redeemed by the shrewd astringency of the author's commentary.

3. SECONDARY

G. R. ABERNATHY, jun., *The English Presbyterians and the Stuart Restoration: 1648–1663* (Philadelphia: American Philosophical Society, 1965). Fills a notable gap in seventeenth-century political studies by tracing the fortunes of the English Presbyterians in the Interregnum. A pity, however, that this study is limited in its scope to the Presbyterians' *political* activities; their *intellectual* crisis is ignored.

G. R. ABERNATHY, jun., 'Clarendon and the Declaration of Indulgence', *Journal of Ecclesiastical History*, XI 1 (1960): an important article, which modifies the thesis of R. S. Bosher (see below) on the role of Clarendon in the post-Restoration settlement.

A. L. BEIER, 'Poor Relief in Warwickshire, 1630–1660', *Past and Present*, 35: one of a number of regional studies which is modifying the Weber–Tawney stereotype of Puritan attitudes to poverty.

R. S. BOSHER, *The Making of the Restoration Settlement* (London, Black, 1951): a valuable account of the capture of the Established Church by the 'Laudians' after the Restoration.

L. V. BREDVOLD, *The Intellectual Milieu of John Dryden* (Ann Arbor Paperbacks, 1956), ranges wider than its title would suggest and approaches some of the intellectual controversies of the time from a refreshingly off-beat angle.

N. COHN, *The Pursuit of the Millennium* (London, Mercury Books, 1957): the exciting historical survey of the links between millenarianism and social subversion.

P. COLLINSON, *The Elizabethan Puritan Movement* (London, Cape, 1967): the definitive study of the organisation of Elizabethan Puritanism. It complements, in an interesting way, William Haller's studies (see below) of the evolution of Puritan thought.

M. H. CURTIS, 'The Hampton Court Conference and its Aftermath', *History*, XLVI (1961): a notable revision of the traditional accounts of what went on at Hampton Court between James I and his bishops. The product of some ingenious research, it prods us into questioning other assumptions about James I that have been too long unchallenged.

A. M. EVERITT, *The Community of Kent and the Great Rebellion 1640–60* (Leicester University Press, 1966), is a good example of the scholarly regional study – Everitt himself on Suffolk, Pennington and Roots on Stafford, are other fine models – which is transforming our view of the Civil War.

J. N. FIGGIS, 'Erastus and Erastianism', *Journal of Theological Studies*, 11 (1960): a pioneering article on Erastianism which has rarely received its proper recognition.

C. H. and K. GEORGE, *The Protestant Mind of the English Reformation 1570–1640* (Princeton, N.J., 1961), denies the existence of discrete 'Anglican' and 'Puritan' wings within the broad movement of English Protestantism. For the opposite view see: J. F. H. NEW, *Anglican and Puritan* (London, Black, 1964). The controversy is to some extent an artificial dispute over semantics; both works are too schematic; and yet both provide interesting material in pursuit of their thesis.

C. H. GEORGE, 'Puritanism as History and Historiography', *Past and Present*, 41, December 1968: an eloquent (but not totally convincing) plea that contemporary historiography of Puritanism has taken the wrong turning by following Weber, not Marx.

SELECT BIBLIOGRAPHY 191

WILLIAM HALLER, *The Rise of Puritanism* (New York, Columbia, 1938).

WILLIAM HALLER, *Liberty and Reformation in the Puritan Revolution* (New York, Columbia, 1955).

WILLIAM HALLER, *Foxe's Book of Martyrs and the Elect Nation* (London, Cape, 1963): these three great works on Puritan ideas have been sympathetically discussed in: L. J. TRINTERUD, 'William Haller, Historian of Puritanism', *The Journal of British Studies*, V 2 (May 1966).

C. HILL, *Intellectual Origins of the English Revolution* (Oxford University Press, 1965), is similar to the Georges' book in that its supporting material is superior to the thesis it is meant to underpin. The thesis – of a link between Puritanism and science – has come in for some hard critical knocks, but the book has a life of its own outside its thesis.

C. HILL, *Puritanism and Revolution* (London, Secker & Warburg, 1958): some marvellously stimulating essays, of which the one on John Mason has most relevance to this study.

C. HILL, *Society and Puritanism in pre-Revolutionary England* (London, Secker & Warburg, 1964) is full of challenging ideas about the nature of Puritanism before the Civil War. A classic.

C. HILL, *The Century of Revolution, 1603–1714* (Edinburgh, Nelson, 1961); refusing to be confined within the textbook straitjacket, it asks some searching question about politics and religion in this period.

MARGARET JAMES, 'The Political Importance of the Tithes Controversy . . .', *History*, XXVI (1940): this article has worn well and still tells us more about Cromwell's evolution in social thinking than many larger biographies.

W. K. JORDAN, *The Development of Religious Toleration in England* . . . (London, Allen and Unwin, 1938) is still the most comprehensive treatment that we have of this important topic, although Conrad Russell, 'Arguments for Religious Unity in England 1530–1650', *Journal of Ecclesiastical History*, XVIII 2 (1967) has some interesting additional material.

MARGARET JUDSON, *The Crisis of the Constitution* . . . (New Brunswick, 1949), is a fine essay on the constitutional assumptions that underlay the political crisis of the 1640s. But its analysis of the Anglican contribution is very ordinary.

E. W. KIRBY, 'Sermons before the Commons, 1640–2', *American Historical Review*, XLIV (1938–9), argues that the fire-eating 'root and branch' ministers were tamer than they sounded. I disagreed with this thesis in an article, 'Episcopacy and a "Godly Discipline" 1641–6', *Journal of Ecclesiastical History*, XI (1959).

W. M. LAMONT, *Marginal Prynne* (London, Routledge, 1963).

C. B. MACPHERSON, *The Political Theory of Possessive Individualism* (Oxford University Press, 1962), has some strikingly original reassessments of Hobbes and the Levellers. These reassessments have not gone without challenge.

On the Levellers, J. C. DAVIS, 'The Levellers and Democracy', *Past and Present*, 40 (July 1968), has some cautionary comments. On Hobbes, a more thorough-going rebuttal of MacPherson's thesis was launched by KEITH THOMAS, 'The Social Origins of Hobbes' Political Thought', in *Hobbes Studies*, ed. K. Brown (Oxford University Press, 1965). Hobbes's importance in the war on prescription is well brought out by Q. SKINNER, 'History and Ideology in the English Revolution', *Historical Journal*, 8 (1965), p. 2.

P. MILLER, *The New England Mind* (New York, 1939), is full of stimulating ideas about the Old England Mind too; particularly helpful on Calvinist theology.

G. R. NUTTALL and O. CHADWICK, eds, *From Uniformity to Unity, 1662–1692* (London, S.P.C.K., 1962): essays by G. R. Nuttall himself and Anne Whiteman are particularly useful on the post-Restoration Church.

VALERIE PEARL, *London and the Outbreak of the Puritan Revolution* (Oxford University Press, 1961), shows that there was nothing pre-ordained about the capture of London by Puritanism.

W. A. SHAW, *A History of the English Church, 1640–60* (London, Longmans, 1900), is still a very useful guide to the religious controversies of the period although he consistently underrates the appeal of radical solutions to many English moderate Puritans in the early 1640s.

L. F. SOLT, 'The Fifth Monarchy Men: Politics and the Millenium', *Church History*, 30, 1961, argues that the Fifth Monarchy Men were a less serious revolutionary force than is commonly supposed.

R. P. STEARNS, *The Strenuous Puritan: Hugh Peter 1598–1660* (Urbana, 1954), contains some interesting material about a lively, if peripheral, Puritan.

L. STONE, *The Crisis of the Aristocracy 1558–1641* (Oxford University Press, 1961). A book on the economic fortunes of the peerage in this period ought to have little to say about the religious moods and aspirations of the time. One could hardly be more wrong if one proceeded on that assumption to eliminate this astonishing book from the reading list.

SYLVIA THRUPP, ed., *Millennial Dreams in Action* (The Hague,

1962): interesting comparative studies of millennial programmes.

H. R. TREVOR-ROPER, *Archbishop Laud, 1573–1645* (London, Macmillan, 1940). An interesting assessment by a young historian on the *social* implications of Laudianism. Ungratefully one wishes now that, as a mature historian, he would rewrite this book and bring out the *intellectual* implications of Laudianism, as he uniquely can.

H. R. TREVOR-ROPER, 'Oliver Cromwell and his Parliaments', in *Essays Presented to L. B. Namier,* ed., R. Pares and A. J. P. Taylor (London, Macmillan, 1956): a dazzling reinterpretation of Cromwell. Much to contest, but that's the point of the exercise.

H. R. TREVOR-ROPER, 'Witches and Witchcraft', *Encounter* (May 1967): brilliantly argued; full of stimulating ideas.

E. TUVESON, *Millennium and Utopia* (Harper Torchbooks, 1964), looks at millenarianism from a different angle from that of Professor Cohn, and has some interesting insights.

J. M. WALLACE, *Destiny his Choice: The Loyalism of Andrew Marvell* (Cambridge University Press, 1968), brings out well the political significance of the Engagement controversy.

M. WALZER, 'Puritanism as a Revolutionary Ideology', *History and Theory,* III, is of value, not only as a forerunner to his book but for one of the most eloquent and convincing refutations of the Weber-Tawney thesis about the relationship between Puritanism and capitalism.

M. WALZER, *The Revolution of the Saints* (London, Weidenfeld and Nicolson, 1966). Not the least of the merits of this finely written book is that it has taken a rather stale truism – about the affinity of Calvinism with modern totalitarian movements – and breathed new life into it. It is not wholly convincing but it is wholly provocative.

MAX WEBER, *The Protestant Ethic and the Spirit of Capitalism* (New York, Scribner, 1948). His attempt to describe the relationship between the two has been subject to much criticism, from R. H. TAWNEY, *Religion and the Rise of Capitalism* (New York, Harcourt, 1926), downwards. Some of the criticism has been pertinent and searching, but a lot of it has astonishingly missed Weber's point (see M. J. KITCH, *Capitalism and the Reformation* (London, Longmans, 1967), for an anthology of these criticisms).

JOHN F. WILSON, 'Comment on "Two Roads to the Puritan Millennium" ', *Church History,* 32, 1963: a modest, brief article full of good sense about the road to the Millennium that avoided social revolution.

B. H. G. WORMALD, *Clarendon: Politics, History, Religion* (Cambridge University Press, 1951): memorable for its re-creation of intellectual life at Great Tew in the 1630s.

Index